SPLENDOR AND
DEATH OF
JOAQUIN MURIETA

————

Pablo Neruda

FULGOR

Y

MUERTE

DE

JOAQUIN

MURIETA

Pablo Neruda

SPLENDOR

AND

DEATH

OF

JOAQUIN
MURIETA

TRANSLATED BY

BEN BELITT

Farrar, Straus and Giroux, New York

For Toby Cole, who insisted

Author's Foreword

The specter of Joaquín Murieta still rides the California countryside.

On moonlit nights one sees him posting over the prairies of Sonora, spurring a vengeful horse; or he may disappear completely into the solitudes of the Mexican Sierra Madre.

Yet his chimerical path always doubles back to Chile. Every Chilean knows this, especially the Chileans of the farms and the hamlets, the Chileans of the mines, the mountains, the steppes, the isolated encampments, the Chileans who live by the ocean, by the Gulf of Penas.

When he left Valparaíso to try his luck in the gold country of California and risk death in the venture, he never guessed that his nationality would be divided and his personality diminished. He never once surmised that his memory would be decapitated, like his body, by men who sought to demean and abuse it.

But Joaquín Murieta was a Chilean.

I have proof. But these pages are not concerned with confirming history or validating fantasy. On the contrary. Between the fantasy and the history of things I have interposed my personal identity. Around it whirls a maelstrom of fire and blood, avarice, outrage, and insurrection.

Joaquín has been the subject of endless speculation; and now there are those who would erase him entirely from the map. A new theory has been added to the canon. They are saying that Murieta was not one, but legion: not one man, but seven. Seven bandits. Seven bands.

That is one way of quashing a rebellion. But I refuse to accept it.

Whoever approaches the truth or legend of this bandit will feel the charismatic force of his gaze.

His beheading is the subject of this cantata. I have written for Joaquín Murieta not only an insurrectionary cantata but a birth certificate.

His identification papers were lost in the earthquakes of Valparaíso or vanished from the land-office records in the gold fields. That is why he must be reborn in his own right—a pillar of smoke or a pillar of fire—as the exemplar of a harsh time, a doomed avenger.

If I have sometimes been carried along on the winds of the fury that carried the man, if my words seem excessive at times, I am content.

Perhaps I undertook this song in the hope of losing myself for a time in the hazards of his lonely rebellion. Perhaps I wanted to share his very existence. For these reasons, among others, I offer this testimony to the splendor of that life and the meaning of that death.

Pablo Neruda

Author's Note

This is a tragic work; but it is also, in part, a *jeu d'esprit*: by which I mean it is intended as a melodrama, an opera, and a pantomime.

I would urge all directors to invent situations and props to their own liking—the costumes and décor that serve them best.

The stars that appear in one of the scenes, for example, might open out like great pinwheels whirling over the heads of the spectators. The Vigilantes (precursors of the Ku Klux Klan) can be mounted on straw hobbyhorses, the clients of the Fandango Tavern can wear king-size mustaches. A rabbit can be substituted for the doves in another episode. Where possible, the stage action may be supplemented by running motion-pictures. A sailing ship might be constantly in evidence in one area of the stage during the voyage of the brig.

The idea of a funeral cortege, which should register with some pathos—a crude pathos bordering on the grotesque—I borrowed from an unforgettable memory of a Noh play I saw years ago in Yokohama, in a small suburban theater, seated cross-legged on the floor, like any visiting sailor. I was overwhelmed by the effect of the funeral procession and have hoped ever since for a chance to communicate the same depth of feeling in a comparable situation.

I have none of the vanity of the professional playwright; and, as will soon be evident, I am aware of my limitations in a strange genre. For the rest of it: I never grasped one iota of what was going on in the Japanese play. I would hope that the spectators of this tragedy might have a similar experience.

P.N.

Translator's Foreword

If, as Valéry supposed, poems are not completed but abandoned, it may be equally as true of plays written in verse that their completion must be constantly reinvented. The play that is written with words must constantly alter its inflection and contend with both the contemporaneity of its audience and the waywardness of the theater as such. Audience and actor are engaged in a continuous labor of revision. Gertrude Stein once suggested that a play is always seen in two dimensions of time: Time Past, in which we savor and engage all that we have already experienced and enlist the total validation of our lifetime; and Time Present, in which we experience a moment of unprecedented relatedness to the drama.

In this sense, all plays are in a state of "translation." The director "translates" the play into an equivalence of his own vision, brings it out of the courtyard or the folio onto an apron, a turntable, a bare set of planks, throws a line of fire between the spectators and the players, shows it in the round, or the three-quarters, or minus a fourth wall, with grapes and masks and cherubs climbing a proscenium, as if to remind us of the mythic origin of our pleasure. The actor "translates" the text by voicing and moving the word and investing it with the physical integrity of his craft. The designer "translates" it by bounding the spaces and devising the ambiance for an action.

What, then, is left for the translator to translate? Everything —and something in excess of all the moving and shaking for which enacted plays are destined. In the first place, it should be perfectly obvious that the translator is involved in a moving of languages—a monumental changing of the sounds that permeates into every function of *performance* and forces an imaginative engagement with all the exigencies which govern the mysteries of theatrical communication: the time of the play, both inside and out; the speed and passion of the actor's sensibility and the audience's involvement; the charismatic authority of the language; and that secret marriage of affinities which makes plays *playable* and touches the "occupation" of the player. In the second place, the translator reinvents the dynamics of the dramatic undertaking: its literal action in the Aristotelian sense of the word: the transmutation of energies into words which order the tension of a total enterprise and fix its somatic and symbolic immediacies: the *dromenon*.

In the case of plays formalized as poems, the translator must reckon with yet another dimension which is the province of poetry itself: with the force that called words from the void and gave language to everything felt and envisioned in the play —the spiritual priority of poetry over every other consideration, insofar as the utterance itself is to be poetry. It is tempting, under the circumstances, to postulate the inherent equivalence of poetry and drama, but despite the long history of their coexistence, a better case can be made for the *antipoetic* character of theater. The record of poets who have deviated into drama does not suggest that plays are the gratuitous outcome of poetry. Everything indicates that the poet is the first to fail at his drama and the last to blot out a line in the interests of the drama's effectiveness. Neruda himself, a self-confessed apprentice (*"aprendiz de teatrero"*), had the good

humor to register his frustration in a kind of curtain speech*
drafted from the safe distance of Isla Negra. There were, he
says, "verses that rhyme as they did in my palmiest days . . .
and dances, with music by Sergio Ortega, and Pedro Orthous,
that famous theatrical director, to make his cut in the pie . . .
urging this little change and that small deletion . . . and if I
protested I was told the same thing had happened to
Shakespeare and Lope de Vega . . . After all, I am only a
stage-struck apprentice . . . I gave in to everything so that
Murieta could ride again."

Splendor and Death of Joaquín Murieta is, geographically, an
American play. It joins two continents together by traveling
northward from Valparaíso, crossing the Central American
peninsula into Mexico, and planting itself on the Barbary Coast
and the foothills of the Mother Lode. Its scope is Pan-
American but its locus is San Francisco, U.S.A., and the weight
of its history is specifically *yanqui*. For Chileans, it is a play
about disfranchised compatriots in a country of rapists and
capitalist bigots. It concerns Latin-American aliens in an
ambiance to which North Americans hold the linguistic and
psychological keys. As "host-country," California makes unique
demands on the plausibility of the language for North American
readers, quite as much as any Californian's play about
Anaconda Copper in Chile would be accountable to South
Americans for the inflection and credibility of its participants.
More than a substitution of one "rush" for another, of copper
and nitrates for gold, or United Fruit for Joaquín Murieta, is
involved in the theatrical transaction. Playwright and
translator alike must reckon with the American *sound* itself and
find an intonation which checks with whatever is idiosyncratic
to the *yanqui* sense of history, his real or imagined vision of

*Por qué Joaquín Murieta. Obras completas, Pablo Neruda, Vol. II, pp.
1133–34. Buenos Aires: Editorial Losada, S.A. See Appendix.

its archetypes: cowboys, 'forty-niners, vigilantes, pitchmen, desperadoes.

Of course, it is possible to dismiss such considerations as false to the spirit of what Neruda himself has quixotically called an opera, a pantomime, a melodrama, a *jeu d'esprit*, a song, a tragedy and an "insurrectionary cantata." It is possible, that is to say, to read *Splendor and Death* nonrepresentationally, as a literal "horse opera" enlisting the conventions of cinematic American mythology quite as much as it professes to adopt the conventions of Japanese Noh drama. A histrionic rather than a historical stereotype of American violence, derived from Puccini, D. W. Griffith and Hollywood Westerns, will serve for Neruda's translators in Germany, Italy, and France quite as much as it appears to have served for Neruda himself. All may be equally quaint—the Hooded Figures (*encapuchados*) enacting their barbaric rites of preemption and genocidal slaughter; the Beheaded Bandit, many times larger than life, speaking out of his cage in a Yokohaman funeral cortege; the choruses of Latin American keeners tuning their laments to the "high style" of neo-Grecian tragedy; the vaudeville turns of Box and Cox, or Laurel and Hardy, in the plain prose of Jack Three-Fingers and Reyes; the rapid-fire patter exchanged by the Gentleman Swindler and his Accomplices in the prosody of Gilbert and Sullivan and the style of the Spanish *zarzuela*.

The *yanqui* reader, however, born to the feel of the cowboys-and-Indians myth, has a right to expect an American "sound" not present in the inflection of Neruda, a sound native to the Klansman and the con man. The "heavies" of an American horse opera ought to display some of the expertise (admittedly a jargon) of Caliban—a true artist in the theater, as Auden has shown us—who roundly berated his creator: "You taught me language; and my profit on 't / Is, I know how to curse." The bullies of Neruda do not know how to curse: they have not learned how to invite a quarrel or fan the passions of a lynch mob in the vernacular: not even the vernacular of the Hollywood

Western. They are not sinister. Neruda is content merely to indicate, with an alien's English: "Shut up! Damn you! Go to hell!" or "Silence!" (one hears the word Spanishly: "*Silencio!*") "No niggers here!" or "You are now in California. Here's no chicha! In California you must have whiskey!"—and doubtless his translators in Italy, France, and Germany will see nothing odd in all this.

These are linguistic considerations bearing on the *playableness* of the play, and as such a concern of the translator who translates for the stage rather than the closet or classroom. To this extent, I suppose, portions of Episodes Three and Four, incidental songs laced with Latin-American place names and spinning their rhythms out of the pyrotechnical patter of the barker, occasional lyrics which must *sing* their way to an English end as they did in the Spanish, may be called "adaptations" of their originals. Occasionally, I have condensed a sequence of lines in the interests of "American" momentum—with, I trust, due regard for sense and continuity. And in one case I omitted a fanciful turn of action—the attempt of the Klansmen to revive their "dead" Kleagle with a ritual dance—where the overload threatened to blow every fuse in the switchboard. Two café tunes written in English and intended for a Black and a Blond Singer in Episode Three I have reserved for the appendix, whence they may be retrieved by both the historian and the producer who chooses to restore them to their original sequence. It is no disservice to Neruda to say that his English and mine do not mix; but in every other respect I have worked for systematic fidelity to the context and spirit of the original Spanish—for a translation rather than an adapter's overlay.

The point needs to be made because Neruda himself in a prefatory note has urged extraordinary liberties upon his directors which might easily seduce the "creative" translator: the right to "invent situations and props to their own liking" ("*para que invente situaciones u objetos fortuitos*"). My own intention, however faultily pursued, has been precisely the opposite: I have opted for the poetry of *Splendor and Death* in the belief that the play as poem, "cantata," song, is the deepest concern of Neruda and carries the total authority of his signature. Indeed, the poem as poem not only preceded the play but is retained virtually intact, with a scant handful of omissions, its symmetry untouched, within the play itself, as a kind of progressive scenario. In Neruda's poetics of tragedy the poem preceded the play by a year and was one of twelve "episodes" or sea chanteys incorporated in an ambitious sequence of "barcaroles"* devoted to Rubén Darío, Rubén Asócar, Lord Cochrane of Chile, astronauts, Paris, Russia, and Latin American earthquakes, as a kind of nautical celebration of the poet's wife, Matilde Urrutia. One such *barcarola*, which concluded Volume V of Neruda's earlier *Memorial de Isla Negra* (1964) and was later transposed into *La Barcarola* (1967) as an induction to his muse, is actually entitled "Amores: Matilde," as if to prefigure the love of Joaquín for the girl of Coihueco. In the laconic footnote to his play, entitled *Why Joaquín Murieta?* Neruda reports, between suspension points:

I wrote a big book of poems . . . I called it *The Barcarole* . . . a kind of ballad . . . I nibbled a bit of this and a bit of that out of my stock of poetic staples . . . and in this book there are episodes that sing and tell stories . . . That's how I do things . . . from the very beginning . . . I can't manage otherwise . . . Well, one day I picked and I prodded, a great cloud of dust arose like the tail end of an earthquake, flying around till it turned into an episode about a horse and its rider and started to gallop about in my verses—very long verses, this time, like highways or thoroughfares . . . and I rode herd behind them, verses and all, and struck gold, California gold with Chileans panning the sand and schooners under a full load of canvas sailing out of Valparaíso . . . Then my wife, Matilde Urrutia, said: But this is sheer theater! . . . Theater? I said to her. And I still don't know the answer.

* *La Barcarola.* Buenos Aires: Editorial Losada, S.A., 1967.

The initiating poem bore the same title as the play, *Fulgor y muerte de Joaquín Murieta*; and the "very long verses"—the most sonorous and Gongoresque in the repertory of Neruda—recall the heroic hexameters, dactylic and anapestic by turns, of Stesichorus of Himera, the great "choirsetter" from whom Pindar is supposed to have learned the grand style of choral oratory. They recur in the play without forfeiting so much as a carat's weight of their original pomp, with all their internal rhymes—often three to a line of verse—intact, ingeniously infiltrated into Male Choruses, Women's Choruses, quartets, trios, duets, or orchestral dialogues in which stanzas are broken into antiphonal choruses for massed speakers and dancers, in Greek forensic style. Thus, the opening stanza of *La Barcarola* also opens the play, as a Prologue assigned to the Voice of the Poet; and the Voice of the Poet constantly recurs to remind us that Neruda's insurrectionary cantata is, at its deepest level, the *drama of the making of a poem*, like Whitman's *When Lilacs Last in the Dooryard Bloom'd*. As in the original poem, the poet is constantly present in his drama of "splendor and death," meditating the occasion of his poem, appraising the morality of his hagiography of violence, vindicating the banditry of his hero, mediating, justifying, disclosing: the theophanic god-in-the-machine of his contrivance. By Episode Five, the poet, considering "the right and the wrong of this Bandit's Cantata," can say: "I call the rage of my countryman just." In the final episode, the Head of Murieta openly invokes the Poet-behind-the-Play as his *deus ex machina*:

What intruder
or friend, tracing the naked truth in the snow,
shall interpret my story or sing it in truth, in the end?
My time is a hundred years hence. My lips shall be Pablo Neruda.

And at the play's end, it is the author of *La Barcarola* himself who steps out, hexameters and hendecasyllables still unscathed,

to pronounce the poet's epilogue, precisely as it was in the
sea song:

You were one of your country's romantics.
Not mine to censure the outcome: a cavalcade fearful and fiery;
or construe its destruction. I only know a brave man went under.
For spirits like yours, no path leads back to an option. They
    blunder,
their teeth grating fire, they burn, they rise like a phoenix,
    then return to their faraway aerie.
They take life from the coals that consume them; the coal
    burns them back to a cinder.

Joaquín, return to your nest: gallop the air toward the
    south on your blood-colored stallion.
The streams of the country that bore you sing out of silvery
    mouths. Your Poet sings with them.

Ben Belitt

SPLENDOR AND
DEATH OF
JOAQUIN MURIETA

———

REPRESENTANTES

Juan Tresdedos

Adalberto Reyes   (Oficinista)

Tres cantantes mujeres

Un Caballero Tramposo

Un Barraquero de Feria   (el mismo Caballero Tramposo)

Un Vendedor de Pájaros

Un Músico Vagabundo

Indio Rosendo Juárez

Encapuchados y Corifeos

Grupo de campesinos, mineros, pescadores y grupo de mujeres
que se suponen esposas o familiares de los anteriores. Todos, con
alguna característica nacional, intervienen alternativamente en
las escenas tituladas coro.

La voz del Poeta

La voz de Joaquín Murieta

DRAMATIS PERSONAE

———

Jack Three-Fingers

Adalberto Reyes   (Customs Office clerk)

Three Singing Women

A Gentleman Swindler

A Carnival Barker   (also the Gentleman Swindler)

A Bird Vendor

A Roving Musician

Rosendo Juárez, Indian

Hooded Figures and Chorus Leader

Groups of peasants, miners, fishermen. Group of women, supposedly the wives or friends of the men. All, with some distinguishing national characteristic, participate alternately in the scenes specified as Choral.

The Voice of the Poet

The Voice of Joaquín Murieta

La voz de Teresa Murieta

Coro de Canillitas

Coro de Tentadores

La acción se desarrolla en seis cuadros:

PRIMERO—LA PARTIDA

SEGUNDO—LA TRAVESÍA Y LA BODA

TERCERO—EL FANDANGO

CUARTO—LOS GALGOS Y LA MUERTE DE TERESA

QUINTO—FULGOR DE JOAQUÍN

SEXTO—MUERTE DE MURIETA

The Voice of Teresa Murieta

Chorus of Street Hawkers

Chorus of Tempters

The action unfolds in six scenes or episodes:

ONE—DEPARTURE

TWO—PASSAGE AND WEDDING

THREE—FANDANGO

FOUR—THE BLOODHOUNDS AND THE DEATH OF
    TERESA

FIVE—THE SPLENDOR OF JOAQUÍN

SIX—THE DEATH OF MURIETA

PRÓLOGO

(Se apagan todas las luces del teatro.)

Voz del Poeta—

Ésta es la larga historia de un hombre encendido:
natural, valeroso, su memoria es un hacha de guerra.
Es tiempo de abrir el reposo, el sepulcro del claro bandido,
y romper el olvido oxidado que ahora lo entierra.
Tal vez no encontró su destino el soldado, y lamento
no haber conversado con él, y con una botella de vino
haber esperado en la Historia que pasara algún día su gran
    regimiento.
Tal vez aquel hombre perdido en el viento hubiera cambiado el
    camino.
La sangre caída le puso en las manos un rayo violento,
ahora pasaron cien años y ya no podemos mover su destino:
así es que empecemos sin él y sin vino en esta hora quieta
la historia de mi compatriota, el bandido honorable don Joaquín
    Murieta.

PROLOGUE

_____

(_With the theater blacked out._)

Voice of the Poet—

This is the tall story of a passionate man:
natural, brave. His memory hits like a tomahawk.
It's time to disturb his long sleep, the grave of that purest of
    bandits,
break open the oblivious rust of his burial.
A warrior who never found his vocation, it may be. I mourn him.
Man to man, we might have talked. I've sweated out History
with a bottle of wine for the day when his regiment passed.
Perhaps, groping in wind, he came by a different direction.
A sunburst of violence drove the blood back into his hands:
a century passed: we still cannot alter his destiny.
The wine and the man are not ours. We must start in a quieter
    time
my compatriot's story: Don Joaquín Murieta, honorable bandit.

CUADRO
PRIMERO

———

PUERTO DE VALPARAÍSO.
LA PARTIDA

(Se encienden todas las luces del escenario. Música. El CORO Y TODOS
LOS PERSONAJES *entran como en una presentación circense.)*

Coro—

Es larga la historia que aterra más tarde y que nace aquí abajo
en esta angostura de tierra que el Polo nos trajo y el mar y la
      nieve disputan.
Aquí entre perales y tejas y lluvia brillaban las uvas chilenas
y como una copa de plata que llena la noche sombría de pálido
      vino,
la luna de Chile crecía entre boldos, maitenes, albahacas,
      orégano, jazmines, porotos, laureles, rocío.
Entonces nacía a la luz del planeta un infante moreno,
y en la sombra serena es el rayo que nace, se llama Murieta,
y nadie sospecha a la luz de la luna que un rayo naciente
se duerme en la cuna entre tanto se esconde en los montes la
      luna:
es un niño chileno color de aceituna y sus ojos ignoran el llanto.
Mi patria le dio las medallas del campo bravío, de la pampa
      ardiente:
parece que hubiera forjado con frío y con brasas para una
      batalla

SCENE
ONE

PORT OF VALPARAÍSO.
DEPARTURE

(The lights come up full. Music. CHORUS *and* CAST *enter in a circus walk-around.)*

Chorus—

It's a long story. It tacks toward us slowly. It begins here
in this bottleneck washed down to us by the Pole, disputed by
    ocean and blizzard.
Here, under pear trees, linden, and rain burn the grapevines of
    Chile.
The full moon of Chile rises on morning devotions: oregano,
    laurel, basil, jasmine, bean plants, and dew.
It glows like a goblet of silver; night brims with its delicate wine.
Here a dark child was born to the light of our planet,
in the still of the dark, a spark called Murieta,
Chile's olive-skinned child, his eyes still untamed by a grief.
Who would have guessed that a sickle of newly born moonlight
Slept in the cradle where a planet sank under the hills?
He wore wilderness medals that blaze on the pampas of Chile
and seem forged in the freeze and the fathoms, for battles.
His body, a plow; his voice, a rebellion; a double menace of arms.
Then a fever flamed out of Chile, gold raced toward the sea and
    the mountains.

su cuerpo de arado, y es un desafío su voz, y sus manos son dos
   amenazas.
La llama del oro recorre la tierra de Chile del mar a los montes
y comienza el desfile desde el horizonte hacia el Puerto, el
   magnético hechizo
despuebla Quillota, desgrana Coquimbo, las naves esperan en
   Valparaíso.

Escena en el Puerto de Valparaíso

*(Proyección de una panorámica de Valparaíso en 1850 según el grabado
de Rugendas. Una banda pueblerina ejecuta una retreta que anima el paseo
en la explanada.* FUTRES Y ROTOS *se pasean. Entre los paseantes,
está* DON VICENTE PÉREZ ROSALES.*)*

Roto primero—

No hay como el Puerto! No hay paseo como éste! Mira qué
   futrerío!

Roto segundo—

Hay que distinguir, compañero. Hay futre y futre.

Roto primero—

Hay tongo y tongo! Colero y colero!

Roto tercero—

Ese que pasa es don Vicente.

Roto cuarto—

Qué don Vicente?

Roto tercero—

Don Vicente Pérez Rosales, el escritor.

Roto cuarto—

Sabrá algo del oro?

The horizon filled with processions, bore down on the Port till
　　the pull of its magic
unpeopled Quillota, ground past Coquimbo, readied ships in
　　Valparaíso.

Port of Valparaíso

(A *panoramic projection of Valparaíso in 1850, as engraved by
Rugendas. A village band playing; the paseo in the esplanade is in full
swing.* DANDIES *and* ROUSTABOUTS *mingle—among them,*
DON VICENTE PÉREZ ROSALES.)

First Roustabout—

That's the Port for you: one big fandango! Just look at them
　　dudes!

Second R.—

Well, they is dudes and they is dudes. You gotta distinguish, my
　　friend.

First R.—

They is pitchmen and pitchmen! They is setups and setups!

Third R.—

There goes Don Vicente hisself!

Fourth R.—

Who's Don Vicente?

Third R.—

I allude to none other than Don Vicente Pérez Rosales, the
　　book writer.

Fourth R.—

Now, he wouldn't be knowing about gold?

Roto tercero—

No ves que es escritor? Don Vicente lo sabe todo!

Roto cuarto—

Preguntémosle, entonces!

Roto tercero—

No me atrevo.

Roto cuarto—

Échale, no más!

Roto tercero—

Ya está, pues! Don Vicente!

Don Vicente—

Qué hay, muchachos?

Roto tercero—

Qué sabe del oro, don Vicente? Dicen que hay montañas de oro
   en California!

Don Vicente—

Todo eso es prematuro. Hasta ahora, solo son rumores dorados.
   Pero si hay oro, iremos a dar una vuelta. A pata'e perro no
   me la gana nadie. Ya veremos lo que dice la prensa.

(*Rumores callejeros. Irrumpe, desde la platea hasta subir al escenario, el*
CORO DE LOS CANILLITAS.)

Coro de Canillitas—

El *Suplemento del Ferrocarril!*
El *Suplemento del Mercurio!*
Oro en California!
Gran descubrimiento!

Third R.—

Like I said, he's a book writer. Book writers know jest about everything.

Fourth R.—

Then let's put it up to him straight.

Third R.—

I jest wouldn't presoom!

Fourth R.—

You can try. What's to lose?

Third R.—

Well, here goes . . . Begging your pardon, Don Vicente . . .

Don Vicente—

Something troubling you, gentlemen?

Third R.—

We was just wondering about all that gold, Don Vicente. Is it true there are whole mountains of it in California?

Don Vicente—

That would be a premature conclusion. I would say that up to now there are only—gold-plated rumors. But gold in the hills: yes, indeed. I suggest we look into it further; sniff things out for ourselves, so to speak, turn up a stone here and there . . . Let's see what the newspaper says.

(*Street noises. Then a sudden eruption, from orchestra to stage, of* STREET HAWKERS.)

Chorus of Street Hawkers—

Read all about it! *The Railroader's Supplement!*

Compre el *Suplemento!*
Oro en California!
El Ferrocarril!
Montañas de oro!
Ríos de oro!
Arenas de oro,
Compre el *Suplemento!*
Oro en California!

(*Desfile de máscaras de los* TENTADORES *en lo alto del escenario.*
Máscaras de texanos, encapuchados, etc. Una gran voz con acento
extranjero desde detrás de la escena, muy amplificada.)

Voz de los Tentadores—

Gold! Gold! Vengan al oro, chilenitos! Gold, Gold!
No más penurias. Todos a San Francisco. Aquí las están dando!
Al barco! De frente mar! Subdesarrolladitos! Gold! Gold! Gold!
Hambrientos! Sedientos! Venid a mí, soy el oro! A California
    venid!
Con el oro se compran toros! Con el oro se compran moros!

Coro—

Subió la carne!
Ya no hay leche!
Queremos comer!
Queremos ropa!

Voz de los Tentadores—

Venid a mí, soy el oro! Hay para todos! Aquí habla la voice of
    California! Aquí está el oro!

Coro—

(*Tirando sombreros, ropas, canastos al suelo.*)

Vámonos al oro!

Here's your *Daily Mercury*!
Read all about the bonanza!
Get your *Daily Supplement*!
Gold found in California!
Railroader's Supplement here!
Solid-gold mountains!
Running gold in the rivers!
Gold in the deserts.
Buy your *Supplement* now!
Gold found in California!

(A *procession of* T E M P T E R S *in masks, from above-stage. The masks represent Texans, Hooded Figures, etc. A deep voice, foreign in accent, behind-stage, greatly amplified.*)

Voice of the Tempters—

Every bit of it gold! Nothing but gold! Come stake your claims,
    my Chilean friends! It's pure gold, I tell you!
There's a full purse for all! Head straight for Frisco, that's where
    you'll find it!
Ship out! Head for the harbors! All you Underdeveloped
    Peoples—gold, there's nothing but gold!
Ye who hunger and thirst, come to me: I'm forty-four carats and
    California's my heaven!
Buy bulls with your gold! Buy Arabian dancing girls!

Chorus—

Meat's just gone up!
Not a drop of milk in these parts!
There's nothing to put in the pots,
and nothing to put on our backs!

Voice of the Tempters—

Coming my way, Big Spender? I'm all gold, and enough to go
    round.

Vámonos al oro!
No pasemos hambre!

(*Las* M U J E R E S D E L C O R O *arrojan al suelo las flores y las pisotean.*)

Al oro! Al oro!

(*Los* C A N I L L I T A S *se incorporan, tirando los periódicos al suelo y gritando con los demás*)

Al oro! A California! Al oro! Al oro!

(*Suspendidos en lo alto del escenario pasan lentamente de un lado a otro, pulseras, relojes, inmensos anillos y alhajas. Todo en dorado chillón. La escena se ha vuelto frenética.*)

Ya se acabó el decoro!
Nos vamos al oro!
Con el oro se compran moros!

(*Durante la escena anterior el* C O R O *arma un bergantín e iza las velas. Canción marinera. El* C O R O *tira las cuerdas que amarran la embarcación acercándola al escenario, mientras cantan. La canción baja gradualmente hasta ser un tarareo. El* C O R O *entra en el bergantín.*)

Canción marinera—

Adiós, adiós, adiós,
nos vamos a un mundo mejor.
Adiós, adiós, adiós,
se va por el mar el navío.
Adiós, adiós, adiós,
huyendo del hambre y del frío,
adiós, adiós, adiós,
nos vamos en este navío,
adiós, adiós, adiós,
buscando otro mundo mejor.

This is the Voice of California speaking! Come get your gold
   pieces!

Chorus—

(*Throwing hats, baskets, clothes on the ground.*)

Head for the gold, boys!
Let's head for the gold.
There's a bellyful for us all.

(*The* WOMEN OF THE CHORUS *throw down their flowers and
trample them.*)

Gold! We demand our fair share of gold!

(*The* STREET HAWKERS *join in, throwing down their papers and
shouting with the others.*)

The lady said gold! Here we come, California!
The gold's ripe for the pickin'. Cut us in on that gold!

(*Suspended from upstage, a slow procession of objects is seen crossing the
stage space: wristwatches, clocks, huge rings, king-size jewelry, everything
flashing gold-gilt. The scene becomes frenzied.*)

No time for fine speeches!
Let's hit all the beaches
and get on with the gold! Bring
on the dancing girls!
No more bowing and scraping!
There's better things shaping:
gold for the taking
and bulls for the rings!

(*During the previous scene, the* CHORUS *is manning a brig and hoist-
ing the sails. A sea chantey. The* CHORUS *casts off the cable and
moves closer downstage, singing. The song gradually fades, till nothing
is heard but a humming. The* CHORUS *boards the brig.*)

Adiós, adiós, adiós,
adiós, adiós, adiós!

(*Sobre los últimos rumores del* C O R O *anterior comienza el diálogo entre
el* O F I C I N I S T A *y* T R E S D E D O S, *que han instalado una mesa, silla y
papeles durante el barullo precedente.*)

DIÁLOGO

Oficinista—

Oiga! Oiga! No se puede entrar!

Tresdedos—

Me voy, entonces!

Oficinista—

No pues, señor, por aquí no se sale.

Tresdedos—

Así es que no se puede entrar?

Oficinista—

No.

Tresdedos—

Ni salir?

Oficinista—

No.

Tresdedos—

Entonces, qué hago?

Oficinista—

Lo mejor es que no salga ni entre.

Sea Chantey—

Goodbye to you, mates.
A better land waits.
Good luck. May there be
neither hunger nor thirst
as we put out to sea,
and may all our farewells
sail us out of the straits
and into the swells,
out of the worst
and into the better.
Goodbye to you, mates.
Good luck to the helm
and good luck to the rudder.
A golden world waits.

(Superimposed on the last words of the C H O R U S, *the dialogue between* T H R E E - F I N G E R S *and the* O F F I C E C L E R K *begins. They have brought with them a table, a chair, and some papers.)*

DIALOGUE

Office Clerk—

Say, what do you think you're doing! Sorry, only office personnel
    allowed here!

Three-Fingers—

In that case, here I go!

Office Clerk—

Sorry, nobody leaves here without a permit!

Three-F.—

Let's see. No one comes in—

Tresdedos—

Y cómo lo hago?

Oficinista—

Voy a ver las instrucciones. De dónde es usted? Adónde va?
   Cómo se llama? Qué quiere?

Tresdedos—

Eso es hablar. Me llamo Juan Tresdedos. Voy a California. Con
   don Joaquín Murieta me voy a embarcar.

Oficinista—

Tiene todo listo?

Tresdedos—

Claro que sí. Tengo pala, picota. Qué más? Tengo pantalones.

Oficinista—

Tiene certificado de supervivencia?

Tresdedos—

Qué es eso?

Oficinista—

Tiene boletín de casado o recibo de concubinato?

Tresdedos—

No pienso.

Oficinista—

Tiene talón de opulencia?

Tresdedos—

Y eso cómo es?

Office Clerk—

You heard me.

Three-F.—

—and no one goes out.

Office Clerk—

You heard me.

Three-F.—

Well, then, what do you recommend?

Office Clerk—

I recommend that you don't come in or go out.

Three-F.—

And just how do I manage to do that?

Office Clerk—

Let me read the instructions again . . . Hmmm . . . "Where is your domicile?" "What is your destination?" "What is your appellation?" "State purpose of this visit."

Three-F.—

That's more like it! Appellation: Jack Three-Fingers. Destination: California. Shipping out with Don Joaquín Murieta.

Office Clerk—

So—you've got it all figured out!

Three-F.—

Shipshape, I'd say, matey! Here's my oar and my peacoat. Did I leave out anything? Bell-bottomed pants?

Oficinista—

Es un papelito rosado.

Tresdedos—

(*Se busca y muestra un papelito rosado.*)

Es esto?

Oficinista—

No. Ese es un boleto de empeño.

Tresdedos—

No sirve?

Oficinista—

A ver qué empeñó? Un violín! A quién se le ocurre! No sirve.
　　Tiene estampilla de impuesto? Certificado de erupción?
　　Tiene carruaje?

Tresdedos—

No, dejé mi caballo en Quilicura.

Oficinista—

Tiene perro?

Tresdedos—

Tenía.

Oficinista—

Tiene gato?

Tresdedos—

No tengo.

Oficinista—

Total que no tiene nada. Déjeme aquí el boleto de empeño y

Office Clerk—

Do you have your survival certificate?

Three-F.—

Beg pardon?

Office Clerk—

Do you have your wedding announcement or the stub of your
  extramarital permit?

Three-F.—

I can't rightly recall.

Office Clerk—

No receipt for allowable opulence?

Three-F.—

Well—what would that look like?

Office Clerk—

It's a pink slip of paper.

Three-F.—

(*Looks for and produces pink slip of paper.*)

You mean this?

Office Clerk—

Certainly not. That's a pawn ticket.

Three-F.—

Well, ain't that just as good?

Office Clerk—

Hmmm . . . What did he pawn? . . . A violin . . . Who'd
  of thought? . . . No sir, that is not just as good. Do you

vuelva el año próximo. No tiene certificado de nacimiento?

Tresdedos—

No soy de Nacimiento.

Oficinista—

Entonces lo daremos por nonato. Esto le va a traer
complicaciones.

Tresdedos—

Le traigo certificado de complicaciones?

Oficinista—

No se me bote a gracioso. Dónde dijo que iba?

Tresdedos—

Me voy con Murieta a buscar oro. Nos embarcamos en el
bergantín.

Oficinista—

Y por qué no lo dijo antes? Para qué me hace perder el tiempo?

Tresdedos—

No se me había ocurrido. Vámonos juntos, si quiere.

Oficinista—

Métale, pues! Vamos andando! Estoy hasta la coronilla con estos
papeles! Timbra que timbra todo el santo día. Con la
miseria que nos pagan. Dónde me dice que hay oro? Dónde
es eso?

Tresdedos—

En California, le dije. Para allá se va todo el mundo.

Oficinista—

Listo el bote! Partimos. Ayúdeme a empaquetar y nos vamos.

have your customs office stamp for dutiable imports? Your eruption certificate? Do you at this time own or operate any vehicle?

Three-F.—

Well, I've a horse back in Quilicura.

Office Clerk—

Do you own any domesticated pet—a canine, for instance?

Three-F.—

I've a walleyed sheepdog back in Quilicura.

Office Clerk—

A feline, perhaps?

Three-F.—

Never bothered with cats.

Office Clerk—

Grand total: no personal possessions. Leave your pawn ticket with me, please, and come back next year. —Oh, by the way, what about a birth certificate?

Three-F.—

Never was berthed that I know of.

Office Clerk—

Well, I'll put you down as a Caesarian section. That means complications, you know!

Three-F.—

You mean I'll have to bring you a certificate of complications?

Office Clerk—

Don't get funny with me. Now where did you say you were going, sir?

Tresdedos—

Oiga, por qué no nos vamos sin empaquetar, mejor. Para qué queremos tanta lesera? Mejor es romperlos!

Oficinista—

Cómo se le ocurre? Se trata de la documentación, de la inscripción, de la circunscripción, de la numeración . . .

Tresdedos—

Y de la transpiración . . . Al diablo con los papeles! Vamos a volver nadando en oro.

Oficinista—

Sabe que me está convenciendo?

Tresdedos—

Veamos cómo vuelan los certificados!

(Arroja un papel al aire. El O F I C I N I S T A tímidamente hace lo mismo. En seguida arrojan a dos manos montones de papeles que vuelan por el escenario. Al mismo tiempo cae de arriba una lluvia de papeles.)

Oficinista—

Y yo que le iba a dar certificado de tonto!

(Se van del brazo hacia el barco, seguidos por un grupo de cuatro o cinco rezagados, entre los cuales va una niña. Todos vuelven a cantar en sordina la canción marinera, que se interrumpe cuando alguien llama a Murieta.)

Uno—

Murieta!

Todos—

Joaquín! Joaquín Murieta!

Three-F.—

I'm shipping out with Murieta. We're prospecting for gold. The brig's in the bay.

(A *long pause.*)

Office Clerk—

Well, why didn't you say so in the first place? Why waste all my time?

Three-F.—

It—just never occurred to me . . . Tell you what! Let's hitch up and light out together!

Office Clerk—

It's a deal, matey! Shake on it! I've had it up to here with all this paper work! Not to mention what they put in your pay envelope! . . . Now, where did you say all that gold is? Just for instance?

Three-F.—

California is what I said. Everyone and his cousin has lit out for California.

Office Clerk—

Oh, my God! Help me pack and get out of here! We sail any minute!

Three-F.—

Got a better idea. Just forget about packing! Who wants to be bothered? Make a clean break of it!

Office Clerk—

That's the craziest idea I ever heard of! What about my

(Silencio. Todos se quedan estáticos, expectantes, salvo la N I Ñ A, *que regresa al borde del escenario y le tiende la mano a un haz de luz que ha caído allí. En tanto simultáneamente aparece en la vela mayor la proyección de una luz verde y blanca que dará la sensación de montes chilenos con viñedos y nieve en lo alto. En el escenario han bajado todas las luces. Al detenerse la* N I Ñ A, *como también la luz junto al barco, se escucha sobre un fondo musical el siguiente* C O R O.)*

Coro masculino—

Creciendo a la sombra de sauces flexibles, nadaba en los ríos,
　　domaba los potros, lanzaba los lazos,
ardía en el brío, educaba los brazos, el alma, los ojos, y se oían
　　cantar
las espuelas,
cuando, desde el fondo del otoño rojo, bajaba al galope en su
　　yegua de estaño.
Venía de la cordillera, de piedras hirsutas, de cerros huraños, del
　　viento inhumano.
Traía en las manos el golpe aledaño del río que hostiga y divide
　　la nieve fragante y yacente,
y lo traspasaba aquel libre albedrío, la virtud salvaje que toca la
　　frente
de los indomables y sella con ira y limpieza el orgullo de algunas
　　cabezas
que guarda el destino en sus actas de fuego y pureza, y así el
　　elegido
no sabe que está prometido y que debe matar y morir en la
　　empresa.

Una voz muy lejana—

Joaquín! Joaquín Murieta!

Niña—

Va.

documents? My inscriptions? My circumscriptions? My numerations?—

Three-F.—

—and your menstruation, maybe? To hell with it all! We'll be rolling in money. We'll swim back on the gold!

Office Clerk—

You know, Mr. Three-Fingers, you've convinced me . . . ?

Three-F.—

Just watch them certificates fly!

(*He throws one into the air. The* OFFICE CLERK *timidly follows suit. Suddenly they both dig in with both hands and mountains of paper fly in every direction. At the same time, papers snow down from above.*)

Office Clerk—

And I was about to pronounce you a certified idiot!

(*They leave arm-in-arm for the boat, followed by a group of four or five others, a young girl among them. All begin a low-keyed reprise of the sea chantey. It is interrupted by a call.*)

One—

Murieta!

All—

Joaquín! Joaquín Murieta!

(*Complete silence. All freeze expectantly—all but the* YOUNG GIRL, *who walks toward the footlights and stretches a hand toward a halo of light, just spotted in. At the same time, a projection of green and white light appears on the ship's largest sail, giving the feeling of Chilean*

(La luz entra en el barco. Oscuridad total.)

Voz del Poeta—

Así son las cosas, amigo, y es bueno aprender y que sepa y
    conozca
los versos que he escrito, y repita contando y cantando el
    recuerdo de un libre chileno proscrito
que andando y andando y muriendo fue un mito infinito.
Su infancia he cantado al instante y sabemos que fue el
    caminante muy lejos.
Un día mataron al chileno errante. Lo cuentan los viejos de
    noche al brasero,
y es como si hablara el estero, la lluvia silbante o en el
    ventisquero llorara en el viento la nieve distante
porque de Aconcagua partió en un velero buscando en el agua
    un camino,
y hacia California la muerte y el oro llamaban con voces
    ardientes que al fin decidieron su negro destino.

mountains with vineyards and snow on the summits. Lights dim on stage.
As the G I R L *and the light come to a halt near the boat, the* C H O R U S
chants to a musical background.)

Male Chorus—

Growing up lithe in the shadow of willows, he swam rivers,
     broke stallions, whirled lassos.
His valor struck fire. He gave wit to his arms, his spirit, his eye;
     one heard
his spurs ring
deep in the russets of autumn as he bore down at a gallop with
     a tinny flash of his mare.
He came from the high places, where boulders are matted like
     hair; from the taciturn peaks and the wind's inhumanity.
His hands held the ordering blow of the river that lashes the
     snow and divides it in fragrant perspectives.
He chose his initiative; his was the savage delight of untamable
     thought, the wrathful and innocent mind
closing in on itself, nursing its fate in acts of incorruptible fire—
     a chosen one
never given to know
what the promise portended, yet serving it to the death.

A Far-Distant Voice—

Joaquín! Joaquín Murieta!

Young Girl—

He is coming.

(A *light enters the ship. Then total darkness.*)

Voice of the Poet—

That's how it was, friends. We must learn what we can,
     distinguish one thing from another, come to know

what the poem knows as I write it. One must tell the song over
    and over, remember a freeman proscribed,
my countryman walking and dying, walking into infinite myth.
I've sung his immediate childhood; our walker has already
    walked far.
They will kill our meanderer. The elders of Chile come close to
    the braziers at nightfall.
They speak as the earth speaks, as the whispering rain or the
    faraway snow on the glaciers.
They mourn a good sailor who left Aconcagua, cut a path
    through the water
where death and gold called with their blazon of voices and
    sealed his black destiny
in California.

CUADRO
SEGUNDO

LA TRAVESÍA Y
LA BODA

(Se encienden las luces en el escenario. Puente de la nave. Sólo se ve nítidamente la inmensa vela. Diseminados en el suelo, apenas visibles, están los tripulantes estáticos y en actitud de avivar una cueca. Avanzan los RECITANTES *colocándose a plena luz en el proscenio y dicen el siguiente cuarteto.)*

CUARTETO

Voz 1—

Pero en el camino marino, en el blanco velero maulino,
el amor sobrevino y Murieta descubre unos ojos oscuros,
se siente inseguro, perdido en la nueva certeza.

Voz 2—

Su novia se llama Teresa, y él no ha conocido mujer campesina
como esta Teresa que besa su boca y su sangre, y en el gran
   océano,
perdida la barca en la bruma, el amor se consuma y Murieta
   presiente que es éste el amor infinito.

Voz 3—

Y sabe tal vez que está escrito su fin y la muerte lo espera

SCENE
TWO

PASSAGE AND
WEDDING

(Lights up onstage. Bridge of ship. Only the mainsail is plainly visible. Scattered on deck, barely distinguishable, are the crew: tableau vivant of people poised for a dance [la cueca]. The SPEAKERS *come forward, grouping themselves in the proscenium spotlight, to speak the quartet.)*

QUARTET

Voice 1—

Bells logged the days. In mid-ocean, with the white sail in
    motion
tacking and veering, Love intervened. Dark eyes in the darkness
    found Joaquín Murieta:
certain as never before, suddenly all is uncertain.

Voice 2—

Her name was Teresa, a girl of the fields and the mesa,
a peasant who kissed with her lips and her blood; what did it
    portend? thought Joaquín. Then the great
wave broke over, the ship moved into the fog, taking lover and
    lover, till love was forever.

y pide a Teresa, su novia y mujer, que se case con él en la nave
   velera.

Voz 4—

Y en la primavera marina, Joaquín, domador de caballos, tomó
   por esposa a Teresa, mujer campesina,
y los emigrantes en busca del oro inhumano y lejano celebran
   este casamiento
oyendo las olas que elevan su eterno lamento!

Los cuatro—

Y tal es la extraña ceguera del hombre en el rito de la pasajera
   alegría:
en la nave el amor ha encendido una hoguera: no saben que ya
   comenzó la agonía.

(*Se encienden las luces en el puente. Cielo oscuro. Es de noche. Los*
T R I P U L A N T E S *recobran sus movimientos aplaudiendo la cueca. Hay*
guirnaldas, papeles de colores, flores, vasos, botellas. Se afinan guitarras.)

Voces—

Una cueca más!

Una voz—

Y un cachimbo!

Otra voz—

A dormir la gente!

Otra voz—

Ya se fueron los novios!

Otra voz—

Vamos a mirarlos por el ojo de la llave!

Voice 3—

Perhaps all was over, he thought; perhaps all was discovered
    again: his living and dying. He waited. Was he fated to fail?
Perhaps all was a marriage: Betrothed, Woman, Wife. He
    married her under the sails.

Voice 4—

There, in the Spring of the ocean, Joaquín, once a tamer of
    horses,
took Teresa to wife, a girl of the pampas. He delivered himself
    to the forces
as the Sea hurls the waves on their courses, while the searchers
    for gold, inhuman and distant, rejoiced and lamented.

All Four—

This is man's blindness. He searches the bright myth of his
    passage. He widens his range
in a ship where Love kindles its furnace, never guessing the
    ordeal has begun, and all remains strange.

(*Lights up on the bridge. A dark sky. Night. The* CREW *are in
motion again, applauding the dancers. Garlands, confetti, flowers, glasses,
bottles. Guitars tuning up.*)

Voices—

One more fandango!

A Voice—

And then a cachimbo!

Another—

We're asleep on our feet!

Another—

Our happy couple has given us the slip!

Voces—

La cueca!

Otra voz—

Aún tenemos cueca, ciudadanos!

Otra voz—

Y tenemos el cachimbo!

Todos—

Venga!

(*En medio de la algazara, los* H O M B R E S *irrumpen cantando la canción masculina. La escena adquiere ribetes de frenética francachela. Atmósfera no sólo de juerga, sino también de ciego desafío a la muerte.*)

Canción masculina—

A California, señores,
me voy, me voy:
si se mejora la suerte,
ya sabes adónde estoy:
si me topo con la muerte,
chileno soy.

Chileno de los valientes,
tengo el corazón de cobre
y llevo el corvo en los dientes
para defender al pobre.
Le digo al que se me atreva
que donde las dan las toman.
No voy a pelar la breva
para que otros se la coman.

El oro de California
lo tengo ya en un bolsillo

Another—

Let's watch through the keyhole!

Voices—

A fandango! A cueca! A cachimbo!

Other—

There's plenty of dancing to go round, fellow citizens!

Other—

A wingding cachimbo!

All—

Hop to it, friends!

(*In the midst of the hubbub, the* M E N *break into the Song for Male Chorus. The scene takes on the quality of a hysterical orgy. The feeling is more than a spree: it suggests a blind defiance of death.*)

Men's Song—

California, good people,
is right where I'm headed.
One lucky turn of the wheel
and we're all newly wedded!
If I run into Death,
then I'm properly bedded!

I'm Chilean clear through,
I've a heart clean as copper.
I carry a scythe in my mouth.
I defend the poor proper!
Them as itch for a fight
will fetch them a whopper.
They'll get as good as I got,
and I'll skin them for supper!

y lo va a desenterrar
la punta de mi cuchillo.
El que se quiera volver
ahí tiene el mar,
el que no quiere pelear
no nació para soldado,
que se vuelva por el mar
nadando entre los pescados.

A California, señores, etc.

(*Un relámpago violento detiene súbitamente la francachela de los*
H O M B R E S, *que se quedan inmóviles. Las* M U J E R E S, *durante la*
canción masculina, han venido avanzando lentamente en un movimiento
envolvente por ambos lados del escenario, quedando de espaldas al público.
Al producirse el relámpago, se vuelven bruscamente hacia él y dicen el
siguiente coro femenino, ya sea al unísono o en grupos o en forma solista.)

Coro femenino—

Ahora la hora en el buque nos canta y nos llora,
las olas dibujan su eterno y amargo desfile:
qué sola se siente mi alma cuando en la distancia se apaga,
mi patria se aleja, no veo las costas de Chile.
Al oro nos dicen que vamos los hombres amados
y los seguiremos por tierra y por agua, por fuego y por frío,
por ello dejamos a la madre herida y al padre enterrado,
por ello dejamos la pobre casita junto al Bío-Bío.
Ay!, negros presagios nos dicen que no volveremos,
que ya no veremos las lomas de Angol ondular con el trigo,
el oro del campo, la luna chilena que ya no veremos,
y tal vez el oro que vamos buscando será el enemigo
que por rodar tierras
y por mala suerte,
nos haga la guerra,
nos lleve a la muerte.

I got it right here in my pocket:
a gold brick stamped with my name, made
in old California. I dug it out of a rock
with the point of my blade.
Them as yearn to go home
can walk back on the waves, if they wishes.
Them as don't fancy a fight
a man with a gun finds suspicious.
Them as go down to the bottom
will swim for their lives with the fishes.

(*Reprise first stanza.*)

(A *violent lightning flash suddenly halts the festivities. The* M E N *pause, motionless. The* W O M E N, *during the Men's Song, have been slowly advancing from both sides of the stage, with their backs to the audience. At the first lightning flash they suddenly turn to the audience and begin the Women's Chorale—in unison, or in groups, or solo.*)

Women's Chorus—

A changed hour sings and laments to us now from the bow of
        the boat.
Waves trace their embittered and timeless procession.
We groan as we feel the great spaces before us: our spirit sinks
        like a candle
when the coastline of Chile, the face of our country, recedes,
        and we sail on alone.
Gold called to our men: beyond lies the gold, say our lovers,
and we follow by land and by water, through the fever and freeze
        of the weathers.
For gold we abandoned the sickbed of mothers, the graves of
        our fathers;
for gold we emptied the hearth of our houses, the shacks by the
        rivers.
Now we read the black auguries. Never again shall we see

(Se retiran las mujeres y los hombres recobran su movimiento agitadísimo, cantando una vez más la estrofa "A California, señores," etc. Una luz destaca a TRESDEDOS *y* REYES.*)*

DIÁLOGO
ENTRE TRESDEDOS Y REYES

Reyes—

Yo estaba más aburrido en la Aduana! Pero ahora me mareo.
   Es mucho mar para mí. Y este casamiento de Murieta con
   la Teresita, cómo se lo explica usted, señor Tresdedos? No
   le parece demasiado rápido?

Tresdedos—

Lo que pasa, amigo Reyes, es que usted es de los despaciosos
   y Murieta de los vertiginosos. Le gustó la muchacha y allí
   los tiene en el camarote muy casaditos y muy tortolitos.
   Y no están perdiendo el tiempo como nosotros.

Reyes—

Tanto mar por todos lados, hasta por debajo del buque. Y no
   se ve la costa por ningún lado. La verdad es que sin
   aduanas no se puede vivir. Ahora mismo me vuelvo a
   Valparaíso.

Tresdedos—

Si yo siempre le hallé cara de certificado, señor Reyes. Pero
   éstas son palabras mayores. Si se tira al agua, no va a llegar
   muy lejos. Hasta la guata de una albacora y de ahí no pasa.
   El hombre cuenta en la tierra, pero no debajo del agua. Lo
   pasaría mal allá abajo, don Reyes. Y no hay oro en al mar.

Reyes—

Usted de dónde es, Tresdedos?

the hills rising toward us, wave after wave out of Angol, the
  waves of the wheat
near Bío-Bío, the gold of our country, the gold moon of Chile.
  Never again shall we see them.
The gold that we seek, it may be, is our deadly destroyer.
It encircles the earth and the air.
Bad luck lies in wait in its path.
It brings us nothing but war.
It promises us nothing but death.

(*Women move backstage. The men are in watery motion again: they
repeat the refrain of the Men's Song: "California, good people." A light
discloses* THREE-FINGERS *and* REYES.)

DIALOGUE:
THREE-FINGERS AND REYES

Reyes—

I admit the Customshouse was a bore. But I can't help feeling a
  bit queasy. This is more water than I bargained for. And
  then there's the affair of the newlyweds, Murieta and little
  Teresa. How do you explain that, Mr. Three-Fingers? A
  mite sudden, perhaps?

Three-Fingers—

Simple enough, my good buddy. You're a guy who sits on his
  duff, and Murieta is a man with no time to lose. He says:
  That's for me, and he goes after her. They end up in the
  bridal suite, all lovey-dovey and very much married. They
  don't let grass grow under their feet.

Reyes—

Grass, did you say? And what about water? Everywhere I turn I
  see nothing but water: under my feet, under the keel of the
  boat. Right now I'd turn in my passage for a rubber stamp

Tresdedos—

Nortino, copiapino, para que lo sepa. Minero. Allá en mi tierra
y entre dos cerros dejé los dos dedos, que ni falta que me
hacen. Con uno que me quede se puede apretar el gatillo.

Reyes—

Qué gatillo? Por qué quiere asustarme, amigo?

Tresdedos—

Cómo que lo quiero asustar, si ya estaba asustado?

Reyes—

Usted cree que habrá trifulca?

Tresdedos—

Donde hay oro hay trifulca, mi señor. Así es esa ensalada. Y así
la vamos a comer. No tiene importancia el gusto.

Reyes—

Cuénteme algo de Murieta. Lo conoce mucho?

Tresdedos—

He visto crecer al muchacho. Pero no hay que equivocarse. Es
un jefecito. Es derecho como un palo de bandera. Pero
cuidado con él. No tolera el abuso. Nació para intolerable.
Yo soy como su tío y como su baqueano. Donde va lo sigo.
Compartimos la suerte del pobre, el pan del pobre, los
palos del pobre. Pero no me quejo. Sabemos aguantar en
la mina. Y el mineral cuando aparece es como descubrir
una estrella.

Reyes—

No exagere, señor mío, no hay estrellas aquí abajo.

and the skyline of Valparaíso. Taxable imports—that's the only life!

Three-F.—

I always said you had a government seal for a face, Mr. Reyes. Since you're talking so big, why don't you slip over the taffrail and drop in? You won't get very far, I can tell you. About as far as a tunny would take you: which ain't very far. Man lives by the soil, as they say; but not under water. Don't think you'd fancy that at all, Mr. Reyes. Anyway, there's no gold in the sea.

Reyes—

If you'll permit me to ask: where are you from, Mr. Three-Fingers?

Three-F.—

From up north, my good buddy. The mines, in case you're interested. Left a couple of fingers back there in a mountain pass somewhere. But I still do pretty fair in a scrap. They's more ways to skin a cat than one!

Reyes—

Cat? What kind of a cat? If that's a threat, Mr. Three-Fingers . . .

Three-F.—

I hear your knees knockin', Mr. Reyes: but don't pay me no mind.

Reyes—

You mean we're all headed for trouble?

Three-F.—

Wherever there's gold, there's trouble, my good buddy. That's

Tresdedos—

Mire para arriba. Se están luciendo como para despedirnos. Son
    estrellas de Chile. Son las mejores. Si parecen jazmines!
    Allá en el norte, en la pampa, en los cerros, la noche es
    más oscura, las estrellas son más grandes. A veces en
    la noche me daba miedo. Me parecía que si levantaba la
    cabeza de la almohada les podía dar un cabezazo y
    se podían romper encima de nuestra pobreza. Cuántas
    habrá?

Reyes—

Por lo menos aquí abajo no hay ninguna.

Tresdedos—

Las hay también, mi amigo, pero hay que conquistarlas. El que
    no sabe aprende, compadre. Y hay tal vez algunas para
    nosotros allá arriba. Mire, esa que le hace el ojo debe ser
    la suya. Y aquella colorada es la mía.

Reyes—

Y la de Murieta?

Tresdedos—

La tiene bien calentita en su cama, en el camarote.

(*Irrumpe nuevamente la canción* "A California, señores," *pero la
interrumpe* LA VOZ DEL POETA.)

La voz del Poeta—

Silencio, muchachos, la luna, la estrella, la noche, la ruta de
    nuestro bajel,
imponen silencio de miel a la luna de miel!

how the cookie crumbles. Them as want cake get a face full
of crumbs.

Reyes—

And Murieta? How long have you known him?

Three-F.—

Since he was no bigger than a bug, I reckon. But make no
   mistake. He gives the orders. Straight up and down like a
   flagpole. Nobody talks back to Murieta. Nobody walks on
   his shadow . . . You might say I was kind of an uncle or
   bodyguard to him, like. Where he goes, I go. We both
   share a poor man's luck, a poor man's bread, a poor man's
   end of the stick. Not that I'm complainin', y'understand.
   We both took our hard knocks in the mines. But somehow
   when the copper comes out—it comes out shining like stars!

Reyes—

Stars—all the way down here, my good fellow?

Three-F.—

Well, just take a look. What do you see over your head? Stars—
   like a binnacle light, winkin' and blinkin' goodbye. Those
   stars come right out of Chile. The biggest of them all: the
   fixed stars, whiter 'n jasmine. Up north, where I come from,
   night gets blacker and blacker on the peaks and the pampas.
   The stars get bigger and bigger. Some nights, it scares me
   to look. I get to thinking: if I so much as raise my head
   from my pillow they'll come at me like a cudgel. They'll
   empty the little that's left in my noggin. —How many stars
   would you say that there are?

Reyes—

From where I stand—not a one.

(Los juerguistas se retiran en puntillas, llevándose un dedo a los labios
como indicando silencio. Bajan todas las luces en el escenario. Cielo
intenso. Noche estrellada. Se va apagando la escena y las estrellas
comienzan a agrandarse hasta convertirse en immensas flores de luz.
Sólo se ve un ojo de buey iluminado de donde salen la VOZ DE
MURIETA *y la* VOZ DE TERESA MURIETA. *Se escucha el ruido*
del mar.)

DIÁLOGO AMOROSO

Voz de Murieta—

Todo lo que me has dado ya era mío
y a ti mi libre condición someto.
Soy un hombre sin pan ni poderío:
sólo tengo un cuchillo y mi esqueleto.

Crecí sin rumbo, fui mi propio dueño
y comienzo a saber que he sido tuyo
desde que comencé con este sueño:
antes no fui sino un montón de orgullo.

Voz de Teresa—

Soy campesina de Coihueco arriba,
llegué a la nave para conocerte:
te entregaré mi vida mientras viva
y cuando muera te daré mi muerte.

Voz de Murieta—

Tus brazos son como los alhelíes
de Carampangue y por tu boca huraña
me llama el avellano y los raulíes.
Tu pelo tiene olor a las montañas.

Acuéstate otra vez a mi costado
como agua del estero puro y frío

Three-F.—

I say the sky there is full of stars: a man's gotta pick off his star.
  Them as don't know their stars better learn, my good
  buddy. One star to a man—all the way to the end. Bet the
  one that just blinked back at you is yours. And that pink
  one out yonder must be mine.

Reyes—

And which is Murieta's?

Three-F.—

He took that one to bed with him. She's down in his cabin,
  warm as a biscuit.

(*Another reprise: the refrain of the Men's Song. Then the* VOICE OF
THE POET *comes up.*)

Voice of the Poet—

Whisper it, lads. Keep it down to a whisper: the moon,
and the stars and the night: a schooner
cutting into the water; a silence like honey, the moon
and the tired honeymooner.

(*The revelers exit on tiptoe, each with a finger to his lips. Stage lights
dim down. An intense sky. A starry night. As the stage continues to darken,
the stars grow larger and larger and turn into enormous flowers of light.
Then only a bull's-eye is left in the spotlight, from which come the*
VOICE OF MURIETA *and the* VOICE OF TERESA MURIETA.
A background of sea noises.)

LOVERS' DIALOGUE

Voice of Murieta—

Beloved, all you have given me, already was mine.

y dejarás mi pecho perfumado
a madera con sol y con rocío.

Voz de Teresa—

Es verdad que el amor quema y separa?
Es verdad que se apaga con un beso?

Voz de Murieta—

Preguntar al amor es cosa rara,
es preguntar cerezas al cerezo.

Yo conocí los trigos de Rancagua,
viví como una higuera en Melipilla.
Cuanto conozco lo aprendí del agua,
del viento, de las cosas más sencillas.

Por eso a ti, sin aprender la ciencia,
te vi, te amé y te amo, bienamada.
Tú has sido, amor, mi única impaciencia,
antes de tí no quise tener nada.

Ahora quiero el oro para el muro
que debe defender a tu belleza.
Por ti será dorado y será duro
mi corazón como una fortaleza.

Voz de Teresa—

Sólo quiero el baluarte de tu altura
y sólo quiero el oro de tu arado,
sólo la protección de tu ternura:
mi amor es un castillo delicado
y mi alma tiene en ti sus armaduras:
la resguarda tu amor enamorado.

Voz de Murieta—

Me gusta oír tu voz que corre pura

Take my heart's dispensation. Inherit my life.
Take my freedom, such as it is: a man without bread or
     pretensions,
owning only the bones of his skeleton, the blade of a knife.

I grew up with no place to go; but I was my own master.
All that I knew was: one day I would sleep at your side:
a dream that I dreamed in the midst of a dream of disaster.
Whatever happened before, all my life was a nightmare of
     pride.

Voice of Teresa—

What shall I say for myself? I came down from the uplands that
     bore me,
a girl of Coihueco. I boarded a ship in the harbor. We met.
Now I pledge you my life, the fate that lies open before me,
the life still to be lived, and the death that waits for us yet.

Voice of Murieta—

When your arms open out, I remember the odor of cloves.
I remember Carampangue. Your mouth turns to me shyly; then
the hazelnut parts in its pod and discloses its loves;
then all the mountains bring me the smell of your skin.

Draw close to me now. Lie down again at my side
as water returns to its bed, icily pure from the pool.
Rise up—and all is made new: my bride
leaves a perfume of wood on my body, I am sunlight and dew.

Voice of Teresa—

Is it true lovers break like a coal and burn to a cinder?
Is it true that love blows itself out in the breath of a kiss?

Voice of Murieta—

Never ask about love. Why question the fire in the tinder?

como la voz del agua en movimiento
y ahora sólo tú y la noche oscura.
Dame un beso, mi amor, estoy contento.
Beso mi tierra cuando a ti te beso.

Voz de Teresa—

Volveremos a nuestra patria dura
alguna vez.

Voz de Murieta—

El oro es el regreso.

(*Silencio. En la oscuridad del barco sigue encendida la ventana del
camarote de Murieta. Surge una canción en coro. Sólo se cantará una
estrofa con estribillo.* C O R O *invisible. Es la misma canción masculina
de la escena anterior.*)

A California, señores,
me voy, me voy,
si se mejora mi suerte,
ya sabes adónde estoy:
si me topo con la muerte,
chileno soy.
A California, señores,
me voy, me voy.

(*Silencio. Se apaga la luz de la ventana.*)

Or the tree how it ripened the cherry? I know something
    stranger than this.

I know wheat growing high in the sheaf in Rancagua.
I have lived like a fig in the leaf in Melipilla.
I learned what I learned from the water, a dimple
of wind on the water: things flow in and flow out and keep
    simple.

So I knew you at once. All my science and learning
is this: I saw you, I loved you. Oh, my only beloved,
you are the heat of the world that sets my heart burning.
Till you came, nothing moved in the world, or was moved.

Now I want the world's gold to wall you within, like a garden,
to keep you intact in your beauty and stand guard in the center.
For you I keep my heart golden, or let my heart harden
till all is a fortress that none but myself dares to enter.

Voice of Teresa—

I desire only the power and grace of your stature.
All I could wish for is the gold of your plow in the furrow.
Your tenderness holds me, as it holds and protects every
    creature.
My love has its castle whose turrets are delicate, too,
and my spirit bears arms that are forged in the fire of my
    nature—
the love that you bear me, returned, the shield that is you.

Voice of Murieta—

I never tire of your voice: it ripples back purely,
it holds the sea to its sound, the sound to its motion.
Kiss me, beloved: and, however obscurely,
I am happy again: I see you and the night and the ocean.
Kissing your lips, I kiss the earth of my Chile.

Voice of Teresa—

Oh, my darling,
we'll return some day to that soil and grow old!

Voice of Murieta—

One way
leads back: we'll return on a pathway of gold.

(Silence. In the darkness, only the porthole of Murieta's cabin remains light. The Men's Song is heard again—one stanza and its refrain: the CHORUS *remains unseen.)*

California, good people,
is right where I'm headed.
One lucky turn of the wheel
and we're all newly wedded!
If I run into Death,
then I'm properly bedded.

(Silence. The light in the porthole goes out.)

CUADRO
TERCERO

EL FANDANGO

(*Luz sobre el* CANTANTE *en primer plano. Proyección panorámica de San Francisco en* 1850. *Es un grabado de la época.*)

Canción masculina—

Antes que ninguna gente
al oro Chile llegó:
San Francisco parecía
otra cosa en aquel día:
sobre la arena llovía
y resbalaban las gotas
entre las calles desiertas
sobre las casas muertas
y tejas rotas.

No había
nadie hasta que Dios llegó,
hasta que el oro brilló
y llegó la policía,
porque el diablo había llegado
y el puerto desamparado
se incendió
con el fuego del tesoro

SCENE
THREE

———

FANDANGO

(*Light finds the* S I N G E R S *on the first level. Panoramic projection of San Francisco in 1850: a contemporary engraving.*)

Men's Song—

Before all the others,
Chile was there:
the Bonanza-under-the-Hills,
with all its bones bare.
The Gate that is golden today
was no more than a bog:
the desert blew into the Bay
and the fog blew into the dust—
dead houses, blind alleys, smashed shingles,
a good place to drown in:
San Francisco or bust!

First there was nothing: then
a man with a pickax to bury,
then metal to sift in the mud,
then the flash in the pan;
then came God
and the local constabulary;

y en el puerto
del desierto
comenzó a bailar el oro.

Pero el primero que entró
y el primero que bailó
en el nuevo paraíso
llegó de Valparaíso,
y el que bailó con ojotas
antes que nadie y ninguno
era un roto de Quillota,
y el que llegaba después
era un negro de Quilpué,
y el que se casó al llegar
venía de Vallenar,
y aquel que se nos murió
era natural, el pobre,
del Norte, de Copiapó:
se cayó al agua salobre,
al agua de San Francisco,
y se murió de porfiado:
no quería sino pisco.

Pero hablar de los finados
no es bueno,
lo que hay que dejar sentado
en este canto sereno
es que aunque nada ganó
el primero que llegó
fue un chileno.

(*Aparece una taberna, "El Fandango." Hay chilenos, mexicanos, peruanos,
etc. En el fondo hay un grupo de "Rangers" con sombreros tejanos. Luego
irrumpe el diálogo que, empezado por los chilenos, se extiende a los demás
parroquianos. Entre ellos, sentados,* TRESDEDOS *y* REYES. *Ruidos.
Movimiento.*)

then the Devil himself
set his torch to the treasure
to dismantle a city
and level a port in the desert—
and, for his pleasure,
set the rocks dancing.

Callous, they say,
to speak ill of the dead!
Like it or not, willy-nilly,
the truth must be said:
the first man to scrounge for the gold
and take nothing away
was a man out of Chile.

(*The tavern El Fandango. Chileans, Mexicans, Peruvians, etc. In the
background, a detail of Rangers, with Texas ten-gallon hats. A dialogue
begins: first among the Chileans; then it spreads to include all the rest.
Among them, seated,* THREE-FINGERS *and* REYES.)

El primero de todos—

Comenzamos al amanecer. Déle que déle todo el día. Algo
    sacamos. Pero en estos lavaderos hay más barro que oro.

Uno—

Hay más sudor que oro.

Otro—

Yo le saqué dos onzas a la arena.

Otro—

Yo le saqué cinco. No me quejo.

Todos—

Vamos sudando, compadre. El oro pide sudor.

Uno—

Y usted, compadre?

Otro—

No me diga nada, compadre.

Uno—

Se siente fregado? Y por qué?

Otro—

Me siento fregando.

Uno—

Cómo es eso?

Otro—

Tengo lavandería.

Otro—

Y yo panadería.

First—

Crack of dawn: another day, another dollar, like they say.
　　Somebody's got to score. All I get is a panful of mud.

One—

All I get is the sweat off my balls.

Another—

Yesterday I come up with two ounces of gold dust.

Another—

I panned five. I'm not complaining.

All—

Nine parts sweat, one part gold, compadre. That's gold for you!

One—

And you, 'mano—you got nothing to say?

Another—

I got nothing to say, compadre.

One—

All washed up, 'mano?

Other—

It's a ditchdigger's life!

One—

How's that?

Another—

It's a laundryman's life.

Another—

I bake pies for a living.

Otro—

Y yo la pulpería.

Argentino—

La pucha estos chilenos! Se la llevan suavecita! Yo soy maestro de baile.

(*Bailando unos compases.*)

"Gringuita, no te escapés, tenés que mover los pies."

Todos—

Es poco el oro y mucho el baile.

Uno—

Y cómo les va a los de México?

Mexicano—

Para decir verdad, voy a decírselo a usted. Apenas sacamos para una enchilada. De cuando en cuando, una pepita.

Todos—

(*Con música de corrido mexicano.*)

Sudando hasta morir,
podemos descubrir
una pepita de oro
como un grano de anís.

Chileno—

Bueno. A celebrar el orito, aunque sea poquito.

Otro—

Mozo!

Another—

My line is fancy notions.

Argentine—

What a passel of pansies! You Chileans got it too good! Me—
   I'm a dancing master for elegant young ladies.

(Dances a few measures.)

"Gringuita, no te escapés, tenés que mover los pies."
   Translated for Chileans: "If you wanna get out from down
   under, little gringa, you'd better move fast!"

All—

Yeah. All this waltzing around—and no gold!

One—

And how's life in Mexico?

Mexican—

To tell you the truth, where I come from, you're lucky to come
   up with an enchilada. And every once in a while, a hot
   pepper.

All—

(Mariachi music)

Sweat it out, 'mano,
till the day that you die:
you'll pan a gold pepper
and get mud in your eye!

Chilean—

Let's have another round! Here's to a solid-gold nugget!

Others—

Waiter!

Rangers—

(*Desde el fondo del escenario.*)

You must say *boy*.

Chileno—

Boymozo! Una chicha!

Todos—

Chicha para todos, boymozo!

(*Los mozos no se mueven. Avanzan los "*RANGERS*" empuñando pistolones. Uno se queda al centro, mientras los otros encañonan a los parroquianos.*)

El Ranger del centro—

You are now in California. Here's no chicha. In California you
    must have whisky!

Uno—

Pero nosotros queremos chicha!

Todos los chilenos—

Queremos chicha!

Todos los Rangers—

No chicha here! Whisky! Whisky! Whisky!

(*Les ponen una pistola en la sien.*)

Chileno—

Boymozo! Un whisky!

Otro—

Hay que perdirlo con *water*!

Rangers—

(*From the rear of the stage*)

We say *boy*, where I come from, mister!

Chilean—

Boy-waiter!

All—

Chicha for all, *boy*-waiter!

(*The waiters do not budge. The* RANGERS *come forward, fingering their holsters. One stops, dead-center; the others surround the seated group.*)

Center Ranger—

You're in California now. We no sello chicha in these parts.
    In California only sello weeskie.

Chileans—

We want chicha! We want chicha!

Rangers—

No sello chicha. Only weeskie, weeskie, weeskie!

Chilean—

(*Feeling a pistol at his temple*)

Boy-waiter, a weeskie!

Another—

You mean: weeskie wit *water!*

Chileans—

Weeskie wit *water*-closet.

Todos los chilenos—

Un whisky con *water-closet*!

(*Los* "RANGERS" *se retiran. El ambiente decae.*)

Reyes—

(*Después de un silencio, a* TRESDEDOS)

Compadre, parece que hay que tener cuidado!

Tresdedos—

Sí, compadre! Salimos de Chile a tomar el fresco, pero usted tiene razón. Hay que tener cuidado!

Reyes—

(*Large pausa.*)

Qué hora será en Valparaíso?

(*Todos se quedan en actitud estática, mirando hacia el infinito. Sin que nadie lo anuncie, surge del escenario la* CANTANTE MORENA, *que canta su número como una evocación, como algo que pasara en el recuerdo de los chilenos. La luz destaca a la* CANTANTE *y baja sobre los parroquianos.*)

Cantante morena—

(*Música de "Barcarola"*)

Me piden, señores, que cante y les cuente la historia de mi
    enamorado
y quieren saber si mi amor fue tal vez marinero o soldado.
Les voy a contar que nací a las orillas de un río celeste
y el cielo era un río con piedras azules y estrellas silvestres.
Se llama Bío-Bío aquel río y tan lejos está que no sé si aún
    existe:
en mi alma resuenan sus aguas: por eso estoy triste.

(Rangers withdraw. All levels off.)

Reyes—

(After a silence, to THREE-FINGERS*)*

Compadre, I see what you mean. We're all walking on eggs.

Three-Fingers—

Yeah, you might say so. We left Chile for a breath of fresh
    air, now we're all walking on eggs.

Reyes—

(Long pause.)

What time would you say it was right this minute back in
    Valparaíso?

*(All freeze in place, looking toward the horizon. Without any warning,
the* BROWN SINGER *strides to midstage and begins singing her piece,
like a lapse into the memory of Chile itself, or an evocation. The light
picks out the* SINGER *and dims down on the others.)*

Brown Singer—

(Barcarole music)

Tell us the story of your life and your loves, say my gentlemen
    friends.
Who's better in bed: a soldier or sailor? It's only a song.
Gentlemen friends: I was born by the banks of a river,
under a sky like a river with blue stones and stars growing wild.
It was called Bío-Bío: but the maps have washed it away.
When I'm blue I remember the distance, and my soul makes
    a sound like a wave.

I hear them at night, blue stones knocking together, blue stones
    in the water.

A veces de noche escuchando las piedras azules que el agua
     golpea
despierto y no veo sino las paredes que ahora me encierran.

Y siento un dolor que me aprieta la boca y que mi alma
     desgarra
hasta que descuelgo del muro la voz de mi triste guitarra.

Y ahora pregunten si fue marinero o soldado, si joven o viejo
mi amor, les respondo: mi amor es un río que corre allá lejos!

(*Desaparece la* C A N T A N T E   M O R E N A *como por arte de magia.
Vuelve la luz. Ruido de un caballo galopando que se acerca y se detiene.
Entra un* J I N E T E *vestido de negro que habla agitadamente por el
cansancio que trae.*)

Jinete—

Saben la noticia?

Tresdedos—

Qué noticia?

Jinete—

Mataron a diecisiete!

Reyes—

Y a mí qué me importa?

Jinete—

Eran chilenos!

Chilenos—

Chupalla!

Jinete—

Y a tres mexicanos!

I wake up and see four walls closing in. I know I'm alone, in my
    grave.

Misery hardens my mouth and claws at my soul. My guitar
    strings
call out from the wall. I strike a sad chord, and I sing.

Now when they ask me: Which is better: soldier or sailor,
    younger or older? I say: Love is forever.
Love flows out and is lost in the distance. My love is a river.

(*The* BROWN SINGER *disappears as if by magic. Lights up. Noise of
a galloping horse coming closer; then it stops. Enter a* RIDER *dressed
in black. His fatigue is apparent through his agitation as he speaks.*)

Rider—

Something's happened. Have you heard what's just happened?

Three-F.—

Happened? What's happened?

Rider—

Murdered. All seventeen of them murdered!

Reyes—

Well, that's no skin off my nose. We all got our troubles.

Rider—

Seventeen of our own. All of them Chileans!

Chileans—

Chupalla!

Rider—

And three Mexicans with 'em.

Mexicanos—

Caracho!

Chileno—

Y dónde fue, compadre?

Jinete—

En Sacramento. Los sacaron de la cama y los hicieron hacer las zanjas. Luego los fusilaron!

Chileno—

Y por qué los mataron?

Mexicanos—

Es porque no somos güeros, mano! Creen que Dios los premió colorados! Se creen sobrinos de Dios con ese color de huachinango!

(Pausa.)

Tresdedos—

El otro día mataron a otros diez! Les echaron la culpa de la muerte de un tal Conley, que era un conocido matador de chilenos.

Otro—

Bueno. Ahí están los muertos hasta mal enterrados. Parece que a algunos se les ven los pies.

Otro—

Ovalle, se acuerda de Ovalle? Fue el único que se salvó.

Reyes—

Ah puchas, Tresdedos! No me está gustando la cosa! No se da

Mexicans—

Caracho!

Chilean—

Where'd it all happen?

Rider—

Up Sacramento way. Dragged 'em all outa bed. Made 'em dig
their own graves. Then they shot 'em all dead.

Chilean—

But why did they kill them? For what reason?

Mexicans—

Why? Because their skins were the wrong color. Because
Whitey wants it that way. Because all God's children got
codfish over their bones!

Three-F.—

A few days ago, it was ten. Then it was a man named Conley,
they said. God give him a mission: to wipe out the greasers.

Others—

And no proper burial! They say you can still see their toes
stickin' out of the dirt!

Others—

Ovalle—remember Ovalle? He was the only one of them all
to give 'em the slip.

Reyes—

What'd I say, Three-Fingers? We're walking on eggs. I tell
you, I've just about had it! Make a nigger outa me? A
customs inspector? I'd show 'em a thing or two back in
Valparaíso!

cuenta de que nos consideran negros? Mejor me vuelvo a
la Aduana!

Tresdedos—

Ya no es tiempo, don Reyes! Ahora no hay más que tener
cuidado!

*(Todos se sienten apesadumbrados. Como una imagen del temor, aparece
otra cantante. Es la* CANTANTE NEGRA.*)*

Cantante negra—
  (Negro spiritual)

Down goes the river
Down to the south
I've lost my ring
I've lost my soul.

Go, sailor, go, but don't inquire
where I have hidden my own heart!
My heart is there there there
in no man's land.

Down go the winds
down go the clouds
I've lost my ring
I've lost my soul.

Down goes the river
Down to the south
I'll never see again my ring, my ring,
I've for ever lost my soul, my soul.

(En la última sílaba del número de la CANTANTE NEGRA, *dos*
ENCAPUCHADOS *cierran violentamente las cortinas del tinglado.)*

Three-F.—

Save your breath, Reyes. You'll need it to walk on those eggs!

(All sit down, in shocked silence. Then two HOODED KLANSMEN *appear on the raised platform used by the* BROWN SINGER. *She's left the curtains half drawn. They slam them together. A* RANGER *takes his place in front of the curtains, with a fanfare of drums, like a ringmaster.)*

Los dos Encapuchados—

Silence! No niggers here!

(No bien cerrado el telón del tinglado, se introduce por su abertura un
RANGER *y anuncia con un redoble de tambor circense.)*

El Ranger—

Distinguido público. Público subdesarrollado! Este honrado
    lupanar, el nunca bien ponderado "Fandango," se honra en
    presentarles el *Alma de California: La Pulga de Oro.*

(Al retirarse el RANGER *se abren las cortinillas y aparece* LA PULGA
DE ORO, *dentro de un gran marco de oro, envuelta en una capa de
terciopelo negro. Sólo se le ven la cara, el pelo y las manos de oro
bataclanesco. Los* BORRACHOS *se lanzan a adorarla tratando de
atraparla codiciosamente.)*

Coro de Borrachos—

Buscando pepitas
para su mamá,
      catita chiquita,
      no busques más.

Venía la catita
por el arenal,
      catita chiquita,
      no busques más.

El gringo te quita
tu pepa, catita,
no busques más.

      Aquí está tu amigo,
      cásate conmigo,

Ranger—

Distinguished and underprivileged audience! As a specialty of
this here whorehouse, the esteemed and inestimable
Fandango, the pride of the Gold Coast, is honored to
present to you this evening The Spirit of California: The
Lady of Forty-Nine Carats, in person, the Solid-Gold
Louse!

(As the RANGER *retires, the curtained platform stage opens. The*
GOLD LOUSE *appears in a huge golden frame. She is totally enveloped
in a black velvet cape: only her face, her hair, and her gold-plated hands
are visible. The* DRUNKS *enter, hurling themselves at her adoringly,
clutching greedily at whatever they can.)*

Chorus of Drunkards—

Picking peppers
for her dinner,
pretty Patty
picked a winner.

> Poked her ass
> in a pepper bush,
> saw a sight
> as made her blush.

Gringo man
in a black silk topper,
picked her pepper
good and proper.

> Pretty Patty
> let's go steady,
> let's get married
> when you're ready.

cocina la sopa,
sácate la ropa,
no busques más.

Catita chiquita,
no busques pepitas
para tu mamá.

(*Durante este número la* C A N T A N T E R U B I A *se ha ido despojando de
la capa y demás vestimentas en una especie de strip-tease, hasta quedar
desnuda y dorada.*)

Cantante rubia—

Lovely boy,
don't talk
to me!
I want to see
your daddy first!
Please call your uncle Benjamin
and your grand father Seraphim!
Lovely boy,
don't talk
to me!

I am so far
you won't believe!

I am as cold
as a star fish!

Don't talk to me
I think because
Your daddy was born for me!
or your uncle Benjamin!
or your grand father Seraphim!

Put the pot on,
light the burners,
Lord have mercy
on this sinner.
There's pickled peppers
for our dinner.

(*During this number, the* GOLD LOUSE *has been taking off her cape,
then all her clothing, piece by piece, in a kind of strip-tease, and turns
into a gilded nude by the end of the song . . . A burst of applause, with
a few deafening wolf whistles. Enter the* GENTLEMAN SWINDLER.
He tries to make himself heard. Another fanfare of drums.)

(Al terminar este número se escucha una salva de aplausos combinados con silbidos ensordecedores. Aparece el CABALLERO TRAMPOSO. *Trata de hacerse oír. Redoble de tambor.)*

Cab. Tramposo—

Y ahora, distinguido público . . .

(Sigue la algazara. El CABALLERO TRAMPOSO *saca un pistolón y lanza un disparo que acalla a la gente. Le siguen disparos de unos seis revólveres. Se descorre el teloncillo. Aparecen los* CORIFEOS *del* CABALLERO TRAMPOSO. *Cada uno de éstos se va a instalar amenazantemente junto a cada grupo de parroquianos.)*

Los Corifeos—

Y ahora, el gran número de California!

Cab. Tramposo—

Vengo llegando de San Blas
Soy el jugador eficaz.

Corifeos—

Es el jugador eficaz.

Cab. Tramposo—

He llegado de Santa Inés.
Soy un espejo de honradez.

Corifeos—

Es un espejo de honradez.

Cab. Tramposo—

Recién pasé por Santa Mama.
Sólo voy donde no me llaman.

Gent. Swindler—

And now, my distinguished and discriminating friends—

(The uproar continues. The GENTLEMAN SWINDLER *whips out his side arms and fires into the air. The noise stops suddenly. Six other revolvers are heard firing volleys. The small platform curtain whisks open, disclosing the* ACCOMPLICES *of the* GENTLEMAN SWINDLER. *Each places himself menacingly and strategically before a group of Fandango patrons.)*

Accomplices—

Ladies and Gentlemen: the sensation of California!

Gent. Swindler—

All my life I've been a rambler:
first, a Mississippi gambler.

Accomplices—

First a Mississippi gambler.

Gent. Swindler—

A rain-maker, a rum-runner,
but a paragon of honor.

Accomplices—

But a paragon of honor.

Gent. Swindler—

I've been shoved and I've been shunted,
I've been deputized and Wanted.

Corifeos—

El sólo va donde no lo llaman.

Cab. Tramposo—

Y cuando estuve en San Melchor
me recibió el Gobernador.

Corifeos—

Lo recibió el Gobernador.

Cab. Tramposo—

Pero al salir de Santa Lucía
se equivocó la Policía.

Corifeos—

Se equivocó la Policía.

Cab. Tramposo—

Me mandaron a San Ramón
tomándome por un ladrón.

Corifeos—

Lo tomaron por un ladrón.

Cab. Tramposo—

Yo les pregunto, caballeros,

(*Se quita el sombrero.*)

si tienen joyas o dinero.

Corifeos—

Si tienen joyas o dinero.

Cab. Tramposo—

Si encontrarán otra ocasión

Accomplices—

He's been deputized and Wanted.

Gent. Swindler—

When I went to St. Therese,
I was mobbed by the police.

Accomplices—

He was mobbed by the police.

Gent. Swindler—

Out in San Francisco harbor
they booked me for a common robber.

Accomplices—

Booked him for a common robber.

Gent. Swindler—

In San Quentin, hauling cargo,
I was diddled by Wells Fargo.

Accomplices—

He was diddled by Wells Fargo.

Gent. Swindler—

I've been shanghaied by a stranger
and mistaken for a Ranger.

Accomplices—

And mistaken for a Ranger.

Gent. Swindler—

And now, folks, them as willin',
I'll take your billfolds and gold fillin'.

de comprobar mi condición.

Corifeos—

De comprobar su condición.

Cab. Tramposo—

Ahora verán:
este sombrero
de caballero
que es el mío
está vacío.

Corifeos—

Está vacío.

Cab. Tramposo—

Aquí no hay nada.

(*Mostrando el sombrero.*)

Ni una mirada,
ni una moneda,
ni una monada,
ni una mireda:
todo está bien,
nada está mal,
y ahora vean
este animal.

(*Saca un conejo blanco.*)

Corifeos—

Un animal!

Cab. Tramposo—

Prepararemos

Accomplices—

He'll take your billfolds and gold fillin'.

Gent. Swindler—

Them what's gettin' should be givin':
a man's entitled to a livin'!

Accomplices—

A man's entitled to a livin'!

Gent. Swindler—

Look very closely,
friends: here's a hat
'll hold ten gallons.
Watch me spin it
out o' balance:
nothin' on it,
nothin' in it.

Accomplices—

Nothin' in it.

Gent. Swindler—

Not a bug
and not a cootie,
nothin' under,
nothin' over—
jest a hole without a noggin,
a kind of haberdasher's habit
and a thing of beauty, mostly—
watch me closely . . .

(*He produces a white rabbit.*)

en seguidilla
una tortilla
original,
una omelette
mineral.
Quiero relojes exquisitos,
quiero comer relojes fritos!

Corifeos—

Quiere comer relojes fritos!

Cab. Tramposo—

Primero aceite en el sombrero.

(*Toma el sombrero y vierte aceite de una alcuza grande.*)

No tengan miedo. Ahora a la luz
este huevito de avestruz.

(*Toma un huevo grande de avestruz, lo quiebra y lo echa dentro.*)

Corifeos—

Es un huevito de avestruz!

Cab. Tramposo—

Con unos cuantos relojitos
continuaré mi trabajito.

(*Se arremanga.*)

Caigan relojes a granel
en el sombrero de Luzbel.

(*Los concurrentes sacan immensos relojes con cadenas doradas, resistiéndose a entregarlos. Los* CORIFEOS *les dan golpes de bastón en la cabeza, de tal manera que, al ser derribados los parroquianos, los relojes van cayendo uno a uno en el sombrero del* CABALLERO TRAMPOSO.)

Accomplices—

It's a rabbit!

Gent. Swindler—

Now we'll try for
something harder:
an omelette
or enchilada
or a fancy
ladies' garter.
First, I'll need some pocket watches.
Any watches in the house?

Accomplices—

Any watches in the house?

Gent. Swindler—

A touch of oil, a little nutmeg.

(He *overturns an enormous cruet of oil into the hat.*)

A pat of butter, a dead louse:
now you see it, now you don't—

(He *produces a huge ostrich egg, cracks it open, and pours it into the hat.*)

Accomplices—

Look at that! An ostrich egg!

Gent. Swindler—

Now we'll fry 'em up in batches.
Any watches? Any watches?

(He *rolls up his sleeves.*)

All in fun, and on the level.
Lose a watch and beat the Devil!

Cab. Tramposo—

(*Cínico, al público*)

Ven ustedes? Entregan sus relojes de todo corazón.

Corifeos—

Sí! De todo corazón!

Cab. Tramposo—

Miren ahora con atención loca,
abran los ojos y cierren la boca:
        en mi sombrero
        batiendo vamos
        con un mortero
        lo que aquí echamos.

(*Machaca y se oye un ruido de vidrios triturándose.*)

        No pongan caras
        tan amarillas:
        si es cosa rara
        de estos relojes
        hacer tortillas,
        es más extraño
        lo que ha pasado!
        Y colorín colorado,
        los relojes han volado!

(*El* CABALLERO TRAMPOSO *y sus* CORIFEOS *huyen por el escenario. Los parroquianos quedan confundidos en gran algazara gritando.*)

Parroquianos—

Maldito!
Agarrarlo!
A pegarle!

(A *number of bystanders pull out immense watches with gold fobs and* *chains, then hesitate to turn them over. The* ACCOMPLICES *whack* *them on the head with billy clubs; as they crumple to the ground, their* *watches land, one by one, in the hat of the* GENTLEMAN SWINDLER.)

Gent. Swindler—

(*Cynically, to the audience*)

A free-will offering, straight from the heart!

Accomplices—

Straight from the heart!

Gent. Swindler—

Open your mouth and close your eyes easy.
I'll give you something to drive you all crazy!
>First we beat up the batter
>in a ten-gallon hat
>so nothing will splatter.
>Then we eat what we got!

(*He begins chewing hard: a noise of ground glass is heard.*)

>Somethin' hurtin' you, young feller?
>I do believe he's turnin' yeller!
>If you find that my ideas
>are a mite extraordinary—
>tortillas
>made of watches and chokecherry—
>you ain't seen the best of it.
>Alagazam! and all the rest of it:
>now your watch is gone!

(*The* GENTLEMAN SWINDLER *and his* ACCOMPLICES *sprint* *offstage. The audience waits confusedly. Then a general hue and cry* *begins.*)

Dónde está?
Por aquí!
Se fue!
A romperle los huesos!
A romperle el alma!
Qué bribón!
Hijo de puta!
Cabrón!
Mi reloj!
Mi reloj!
Mi reloj!
Mi reloj!

(*Todos se precipitan hacia el escenario, pero en el momento de subir,
sale del cortinaje un grupo de* ENCAPUCHADOS *que, armas en mano,
los detienen. De inmediato comienzan a golpear a los* PARROQUIANOS
y a destruir el local.)

Encapuchados—

Shut up! Damn you!
Go to hell!

Gritos—

Mi reloj!
Mi reloj!

Un Encapuchado—

There is no reloj!
Here you have it.

(*Golpea en la cabeza a un mexicano con la porra.*)

(*Una mujer rompe una guitarra en la cabeza de un* ENCAPUCHADO.
Éstos reducen a escombros el local. Quedan mesas rotas, las sillas tiradas.

Patrons—

After him!
String him up on a tree!
Tar and feather him!
Damn him!
After him!
Tether him!
I'll break every bone in his body!
I'll skin him alive!
Bastard! Lemme at 'im!
Let's all take him on!
Gimme my watch!
My gold-plated watch!
Gimme my granddaddy's ticker!
He went thataway!
No, thisaway!
Big-city slicker!

Son of a bitch! He's gone!

(*All rush toward the platform stage. Just as they are about to swarm over it, a cordon of* HOODED FIGURES *stops them at gunpoint. They wade into the* PATRONS, *whacking them with clubs and smashing away at everything in sight. In the general melee, cries are heard.*)

Hooded F.—

Serve you all right! Sad sacks! Suckers!
You all had it coming!
Shut up and take off! On your way, motherfuckers!

Cries—

Pinche tu madre! Cabrón! Sons of bitches!
Call out the militia!
He's run off with our watches!

Durante todo este tiempo se oirá un ruido de vidrios quebrándose. Algunos cuerpos inermes en el suelo. Los ENCAPUCHADOS *beben en el mesón.*)

Encapuchado 1—

Every thing, all right!

Encapuchado 2—

I thin so.

Encapuchado 3—

Let us see the relojes.

Encapuchado 4—

(*Se levanta el capuchón, apareciendo la cabeza sonriente del* CABALLERO TRAMPOSO. *Saca de sus faltriqueras los enormes relojes dorados, repartiéndolos entre los* ENCAPUCHADOS *parsimoniosamente.*)

One . . .
Two . . .
Three . . .
Four . . .
Five . . .
Six . . .
Seven . . .
etc. . . .
etc. . . .

(*Se van con lentitud. En el suelo se levanta una cabeza, luego otra.*)

Reyes—

Nos volvemos a Chile, compadre?

Hooded F.—

We're all here to please ye!
We'll grease your wheels good!
Rub your face in it, greaser!

(*He bangs a Mexican on the head with a blackjack. A woman smashes a guitar over a Klansman's head. They tear the place to pieces till nothing is left but broken tables and overturned chairs. Through it all, a noise of splintering glass. Inert bodies litter the floor. The* HOODED FIGURES *resume their drinking at the bar.*)

Hooded F. 1—

Everything roses?

Hooded F. 2—

All hunky-dory!

Hooded F. 3—

What's the take? How many *re-ló-hes*?

Hooded F. 4—

(*Lifts hood, to reveal the smiling face of the* GENTLEMAN SWINDLER. *He digs into his pockets and pulls out the enormous gold watches, dividing them covetously among his fellow Klansmen.*)

One . . .
Two . . .
Three . . .
Four . . .
Five . . .
Six . . .
Seven . . .
etc. . . .
etc. . . .

Tresdedos—

No hay caso, compañero. Nos quedamos! Le echamos para
   adelante!

(*Desde este instante* T R E S D E D O S *aparecerá con un ojo vendado hasta
el final de la obra, es decir, con un parche negro sobre un ojo.*)

(They leave slowly. Behind them, on the floor, one head raises itself, then a second.)

Reyes—

Got a return ticket to Chile, compadre?

Three-F.—

No return trips for me! No more walking on eggs! Right on!
    is the word for us, 'mano!

(From this moment on, THREE-FINGERS appears with one bandaged eye—that is, a black patch over one eye.)

CUADRO
CUARTO

LOS GALGOS Y
LA MUERTE DE TERESA

Voz del Poeta—

Husmeando la tierra extranjera desde el alba oscura
hasta que rodó en la llanura la noche en la hoguera,
Murieta olfatea la veta escondida galopa y regresa
y toca en secreto la piedra partida, la rompe o la besa,
y es su decisión celestial encontrar el metal y volverse inmortal.
Y buscando el tesoro sufre angustia mortal y se acuesta cubierto
    de lodo.
Con arena en los ojos, con manos sangrantes, acecha la gloria
    del oro
y no hay en la tierra distante tan valiente y atroz caminante.
Ni sed ni serpiente acechante detienen sus pasos.
Bebió fiebre en su vaso y no pudo la noche nevada
cortar su pisada. Ni duelos ni heridas pudieron con él.
Y cuando cayó siete veces, sacó siete vidas,
y siguió de noche y de día el chileno montado en su claro corcel.

Detente! le dice la sombra, pero el hombre tenía su esposa
esperando en la choza, y seguía por la California dorada
picando la roca y el barro con la llamarada
de su alma enlutada, que busca en el oro encontrar la alegría

SCENE
FOUR

THE BLOODHOUNDS AND
THE DEATH OF TERESA

Voice of the Poet—

Nosing a foreigner's earth in the dark of the dawn
till night circled the uplands and set them aflame, Murieta
followed the scent of the ore in the vein, spurred on, doubled
    back,
touched invisible secrets, drove a track toward the metal, and
    kissed it.
His single desire was to enter a heaven of gold and come back
    immortal.
He toiled toward the treasure in the sweat of his spirit, humbled
    himself in the mud.
Sand-blinded, fingernails bloody, he bided his time in his
    ambush,
stalking a glory of gold—rashest of seekers, the most atrocious
    and distant.
Nothing—not drought or the sting of the serpent in hiding—
    dismayed him.
He drank down the glass of his fever and the frost of the
    night,
yielding nothing, esteeming his wounds and his passion as
    nothing.

que Joaquín Murieta quería para repartirlo volviendo a su tierra.

Pero lo esperó la agonía, y se halló de repente cubierto de oro y de guerra.

Coro—

Hirvió con el oro encontrado la furia y subió por los montes.
El odio llenó el horizonte con manchas de sangre y lujuria.
Y el viento delgado cambió su vestido ligero y su voz transparente
y el yanqui vestido de cuero y capucha buscó al forastero.

(*Una luz descubre en el centro del escenario a un grupo de* ENCAPUCHADOS. *Están realizando una especie de rito con un ceremonial a la vez lúgubre y grotesco.*)

Uno—

Quién es el padre?

Los Galgos—

El oro.

Uno—

Quién es el hijo?

Los Galgos—

El oro.

Uno—

Quiénes somos nosotros?

Los Galgos—

Los dueños del oro!

Seven times he sank to his knees and lived his life seven times
    over,
pure and unspent in the saddle, a horseman from Chile.

Relent! said the shadow. He remembered a woman awaiting
his step on the threshold, and cut through a gold California,
slashing away at the flint and the silt, striking fire
from his spirit's deprival, cutting the lode for the ore
of a happy arrival: the bonanza that would lead back to Chile.

But his portion was anguish. His lot overtook him, a mirage in
    the quicksand: and war.

(*Lights up on stage-center. An aerie of* HOODED KLANSMEN. *They
are engaged in performing a kind of ritual, in a ceremony at once grotesque
and lugubrious.*)

One—

And who is the Father?

Bloodhounds—

Gold is the Father.

One—

Who is the Son?

Bloodh.—

And Gold is the Son.

Todos—

Amén.

Uno—

Dios está con los indios?

Los Galgos—

Dios les quitó estas tierras!

Uno—

Y qué hizo con ellas?

Los Galgos—

Fueron para nosotros!

Uno—

Nuestro profeta Sullivan lo ha dicho:

Todos—

"Es nuestro absoluto destino extendernos hasta hacernos
    dueños de todo el continente que la Providencia nos ha
    entregado para el gran experimento de la libertad."

(*Mientras lo dicen en castellano se proyecta en panorámica el facsímil
del manifiesto en inglés.*)

Los Galgos—

Indios y mestizos!

Uno—

Quiénes son los mexicanos?

Los Galgos—

Quiénes son los chilenos?

One—

Who are the Elect?

Bloodh.—

None but Ourselves: the Lords and the Masters of Gold.

All—

Amen.

One—

Is God with the Indians?

Bloodh.—

He drave them forth from the Land.

One—

What is his Dread Dispensation?

Bloodh.—

He delivered them into our hands to be scourged.

One—

And what is the Wisdom of Sullivan, what says our Master?

All—

"It is our resolute Destiny to extend all our properties, to
    humble the whole of the Continent given to us by our
    God for his Noble Experiment: a land's liberation."

(*While they are speaking in English, a panoramic reproduction of the
Manifesto in Spanish is projected.*)

Bloodh.—

Cleanse ye of the half-breed and Indian, and be saved!

Uno—

Indios y mestizos!

Los Galgos—

Cuál es nuestro deber?

Uno—

Mandarlos al diablo!

Todos—

To hell! To hell!

Uno—

Quemarlos!

Otro—

Ahorcarlos!

(*Arde una cruz.*)

(*Se prosternan y colocan en forma ritual. Las capuchas con formas de chacales y galgos.*)

Uno—

Sólo la raza blanca!

Todos—

Somos la Gran Jerarquía. Los Galgos Rubios de California! Sólo la raza blanca!

(*Se retiran.*)

Canción femenina—

Ya parte el galgo terrible

One—

How shall we know they are Mexicans?

Bloodh.—

How shall we know they are Chileans?

One—

All are half-breeds or Indians: all are evil.

Bloodh.—

Harrow them back to their hells!

All—

Deliver them back to the Devil!

One—

Burn them!

Others—

Strangle them till they are dead!

(*A cross is lit.*)

(*They prostrate themselves with ritual austerity. Their hoods have the faces of jackals and bloodhounds.*)

One—

The White Race forever! There is only one!

All—

One Domination, one Throne, and one Power! The Blond
    Bloodhounds of California! There is only one!

(*Exit slowly.*)

a matar niños morenos:
ya parte la cabalgata,
la jauría se desata
exterminando chilenos:
y con el rifle en la mano
disparan al mexicano
y matan al panameño
en la mitad de su sueño.
Ay, qué haremos!
Buscan la sangre y el oro
los lobos de San Francisco,
apalean las mujeres
y queman los cobertizos
y para qué nos vinimos
de nuestro Valparaíso!
Maldita sea la hora
y el oro que se deshizo!
Vienen a matar chilenos.
Ay, qué haremos! Ay, qué haremos!

Coro femenino—

Los duros chilenos reposan cuidando el tesoro, cansados del
     oro y la lucha.
Reposan, y en sueños regresan, y son otra vez labradores,
     marinos, mineros.
Reposan los descubridores y llegan envueltos en sombra los
     encapuchados.
Se acercan de noche los lobos buscando el dinero
y en los campamentos muere la picota porque en desamparo
se escucha un disparo y muere un chileno cayendo del sueño.
Los perros aúllan. La muerte ha cambiado el destierro.

(*Proyección de* L A V A D E R O S *en el panorama. Entran los buscadores
de oro con sus herramientas y mientras cantan trabajan.*)

Women's Song—

This is our Terror. The Bloodhounds have gathered in packs
to kill off the Brown and the Red and murder the Blacks.
The bloody safari is on:
the cages are open, the jackals are gone.
The rifle is raised. The barrel whirls in the gun.
We suffer the long degradation of Chile again.
They fire on the Mexican, sweep
over the sleep of the lost Panamanian.
Ay! What is it we do? What have we done!
Our hovels are leveled to ash.
For our women, the gun butt and lash.
For this—the cutthroat, the con man, the robber—
we left Valparaíso, turned our backs on the Harbor.
Cursed be the day! A curse on the hour
the gold glinted out of the lode and shone in the ore!
Ay! The anguish of Chile! Ay, for the whip and the gun!
Ay! What is it we do? Ay! What have we done!

Women's Chorus—

A freeman from Chile lies down by his treasure, weary of
    bloodshed, weary of gold.
He sleeps by his treasure, and dreams himself home: he is
    farmer, miner, or sailor.
He is sleeping explorer. The Hooded Ones move out of the
    shadow:
the Scavengers smell out the gold and come closer.
A sentry falls in the sleeping encampment. A volley is heard
in a void. A Chilean drops, midway in his dream.
A howling of dogs. Death has ended his exile. The long hunt is
    over.

(*Panoramic slide:* PROSPECTORS *panning for gold. Enter* OTHERS
*with picks, hammers, pans, sieves, etc. They begin the panning routine
and sing as they work.*)

Coro de los lavadores—

Buscando buscando buscando
pasamos esta vida perra
lavando lavando lavando
metidos en barro y arena
el oro reluce en el agua
el oro se esconde en la tierra
buscando buscando buscando
con hambre con fiebre con pena
lavando lavando lavando
sin patria sin Dios sin estrella
y el oro se va con los ricos
y sigue la misma miseria.

(*Se repiten las frases del fandango, pero con acento triste.*)

El primero de todos—

Comenzamos al amanecer. Déle que déle todo el día. Algo
    sacamos. Pero en estos lavaderos hay más barro que oro.

Uno—

Hay más sudor que oro.

Otro—

Yo le saqué dos onzas a la arena.

Otro—

Yo le saqué cinco. No me quejo.

Todos—

Vamos sudando, compadre. El oro pide sudor.

(*Entran los* GALGOS.)

Chorus of Panners and Prospectors—

Scrub, scrounge, scrape:
it's a dog's life, a sellout, a bust.
Sift it out, wash it out, rinse it
away: the grime clings to us,
we are caught in the mud and the dust.
Somewhere gold flashes back in the water,
somewhere gold waits under the crust.
For us: only scraping and scrounging and scrubbing.
Fever and hunger and sores.
No land of our own, no God, and no stars.
Gold goes to gold. For us, nothing will budge.
The poor man in his misery gets sludge.

(*The Fandango words are repeated: but the inflection this time is mournful.*)

One—

Crack of dawn: another day, another dollar, like they say.
    Somebody's got to score. All I get is a panful of mud.

Other—

All I get is the sweat off my balls.

Other—

Yesterday I come up with two ounces of gold dust.

Other—

I panned five. I'm not complaining.

All—

Nine parts sweat, one part gold, compadre. That's gold for you!

(*Enter the* BLOODHOUNDS.)

Galgo—

Y ustedes que hacen aquí? Son ciudadanos norteamericanos?
No conocen la ley?

Chileno—

La ley del embudo? Sí, la conocemos. Poquito para nosotros,
todito para ustedes!

Galgo—

Tienen que largarse! No estamos en México. Ésta es tierra de
la Unión.

Chileno—

La tierra es de los que la trabajan. Y aquí somos nosotros los
que sudamos lavando arena.

Galgo—

Ya lo saben. No queremos negros ni chilenos por aquí. Ni
mexicanos. Esta no es tierra mexicana. Si siguen aquí se
van a enfermar.

Mexicano—

Mexicanos nacimos y mexicanos somos. Y a mucho honor, señor
gringo. Estas tierras se bautizaron con sudor mexicano. Se
llaman Tejas y San Francisco y Zamora.

Otro—

Se llaman Chapanal y Santa Cruz, San Diego, Calaveras.

Otro—

Se llaman Los Coyotes, San Luis Obispo, Arroyo Cantova.

Otro—

Camula, Buenaventura.

Bloodh.—

Jest what do you fellers reckon you're up to? Got yer
    citizenship papers handy? Or mebbe you're jest natural-
    born citizens of the U-nited States of America. We got
    laws in this land!

Chilean—

You mean the law of the land office and the pitchmen: all for
    me and whatever's left over for you? Sure, mister, we know
    the law.

Bloodh.—

If you take my advice, you'll git off yer asses real quiet and git
    lost. This ain't the U-nited States of Mexico, you know!
    This here is the U-nited States of America. This is Uncle
    Sam's territory. This is the Union.

Chilean—

Where we come from, the soil belongs to the people who work
    it. And just now it's our sweat that's working this sand.

Bloodh.—

Listen good, greaser. We don't fancy niggers and Chileans
    here. We don't take to Mexicans. Mexico's down yonder
    somewhere, over the border. Now, make tracks! Git back
    where you come from. It'll be a sight healthier!

Mexican—

Right here is where I come from, Señor Gringo. I'm proud to
    tell you I'm Mexican-born and hope to die Mexican.
    Didn't nobody tell you, Señor Gringo, that the soil we're
    both standing on was baptized with Mexican sweat? They
    call it Tejas, San Francisco, Zamora in Mexican.

Otro—

San Gabriel, Sacramento.

Mexicano—

Se llama como Sonora, como Cuernavaca.

Chileno—

Como Valparaíso, como Chillán Viejo.

Mexicano—

Dígame, pues, si estos nombres son gringos o cristianos?

Galgo—

Se llenan la cabeza de nombres, de palabras . . .

Chileno—

Y ustedes se llenan de dólares.

Galgo—

Aquí se acaba la discusión. Los nativos fuera de aquí! La guerra
   la ganamos nosotros! Debemos enseñarles lo que es la
   libertad!

Todos los Galgos—

América for the Americans!

Chileno—

Qué dicen? Qué gritan?

Mexicano—

Dicen: "América para los norteamericanos!"

Galgo—

Y este trapo? Quién lo puso aquí?

Other—

They call it Chapanal, Santa Cruz, San Diego, Calaveras: that's
   Mexican for "skulls."

Other—

Los Coyotes, San Luis Obispo, Arroyo Cantova.

Other—

Camula, Buenaventura—that's Good Luck in Mexican.

Other—

San Gabriel, Sacramento.

Mexican—

They call it Sonora in Mexico. They call it Cuernavaca.

Chilean—

In Chile, it's Chillán Viejo or Valparaíso: like you say, the
   Valley of Paradise.

Mexican—

Man to man, tell me, compadre: does that sound like gringo—
   or Christian?

Bloodh.—

(*After a pause.*)

Sounds like a mouthful of names and foreigners' talk. Nothin
   but words on a map . . . Anyhow, school's out, amigo.
   It's recess time now . . . Now you git yer ass out of this
   schoolhouse! We don't take lessons from foreigners here!
   . . . It says further on in my history book that they was
   a war, and we won it . . . Wanna real lesson in liberty?
   Free's free and bullshit is bullshit!

Chileno—

No es un trapo. Soy chileno. Es mi banderita.

Los Galgos—

A sacarla. Es bandera de nativos!

Chileno—

Y quién la ha prohibido?

Los Galgos—

Nosotros! Los blancos! Los galgos! Han oído? A sacar la
    bandera!

(*Hacen ademán de arriarlas.*)

(*Sacan los corvos.*)

Chilenos—

Así es que es así la cosa?

(*Gresca general. Un disparo hace arder la bandera convirtiéndola en una
antorcha. Los* G A L G O S *se retiran perseguidos por dos* L A T I N O -
A M E R I C A N O S.)

Voz del Poeta—

Y los asesinos en su cabalgata mataron la bella, la esposa
de mi compatriota Joaquín. Y la canta por eso el poeta.
Salió de la sombra Joaquín Murieta sin ver que una rosa de
    sangre tenía
en un seno su amada y yacía en la tierra extranjera su amor
    destrozado.
Pero al tropezar en su cuerpo tembló aquel soldado
y besando su cuerpo caído, cerrando los ojos de aquella que
    fue su rosal y su estrella,

All Bloodh.—

America fer them that was born here. America for the
    Americans!

Chilean—

What's that he's saying?

Mexican—

He just said: all America for North Americans.

Bloodh.—

(*Approaches a small flag stuck in a hummock.*)

And what's this rag supposed to mean? Who stuck this white-
    and-green snot rag up here?

Chilean—

That rag, 'mano, is the flag of the Republic of Chile.

Bloodh.—

We don't take kindly to foreigners' flags in this country.
    They's only one flag in this country.

Chilean—

You mean there's a law against Chile?

Bloodh.—

Betcher ass! We just passed it. This is white folk's country,
    compadre. And we happen to be *it*. Ever hear tell of the
    Benevolent Order of Bloodhounds? We make the laws
    like we like 'em. Now heist that snot rag offa that stick!

(*They move toward the flag.*)

Chilean—

If that's how you want it—

juró estremecido matar y morir persiguiendo al injusto,
    protegiendo al caído.
Y es así como nace un bandido que el amor y el honor
    condujeron un día
a encontrar el dolor y perder la alegría y perder mucho más
    todavía:
a jugar, a morir, combatiendo y vengando una herida
y dejar sobre el polvo del oro perdido su vida y su sangre vertida.

(*Escena: El frontis del rancho de Murieta. Entran dos* H O M B R E S, *uno encapuchado y otro de sombrero tejano. Golpean a la puerta de la casa.*)

Voz de Teresa—

Quién es?

(*Teresa habla desde adentro. No abrirá la puerta. Los* H O M B R E S *no responden. Se mueven sigilosamente, examinando la manera de entrar en la casa. Golpean de nuevo.*)

Voz de Teresa—

Quién es? Qué pasa?

Encapuchado—

Mister Murieta?

Voz de Teresa—

No está Joaquín! Se fue a los lavaderos! Aquí no está!

Encapuchado—

Very well!

(*Se arrojan contra la puerta, que derriban a empujones y patadas. Entran en la casa. Ruidos, quebrazón.*)

(General free-for-all. The flag is picked off with a volley of bullets and burns like a torch. Then the B L O O D H O U N D S *turn tail.)*

(Exit B L O O D H O U N D S, *pursued by* L A T I N A M E R I C A N S.*)*

Voice of the Poet—

So the Posse rides on . . . Lashing their horses, the Killers
     went on with their murders, till they struck at the life
of my countrywoman, the wife of Joaquín, Teresa Murieta.
It's a very old song. Joaquín, coming out of the shadows, never
     guessed
his love lay defiled on a foreigner's soil, with a nosegay of blood
     on her breast.
His spurs first caught in the weight of her hair; then he
     trembled. He
dropped to his knees, kissed her eyes closed, swore by the roses
     and stars:
"Whatever is fallen or fouled or betrayed, I will redress in her
     name!"
Then he rose up, a bandit, committed in honor and love to wipe
     out his shame.
Every joy vanished, says the Poem: face to face with his sorrow,
     wild
with his loss, he paid out his lifetime, avenging, opposing, till
     the wound of her dying was healed
and there in the mud and the gold his blood and his guts were
     spilled.

(Scene: Façade of Murieta's ranch. Enter two M E N, *one hooded, the other in a Texan hat. They bang at the door.)*

Voice of Teresa—

Who's there? What do you want?

Voz de Teresa—

Socorro! Socorro! Asesinos!

(*Calla su voz. Uno de los atacantes, el de sombrero tejano, se asoma a la puerta y llama con un silbato. Acuden seis o siete encapuchados y tejanos.*)

Tejano—

Come on!

(*Entran todos. Continúa el salvaje ruido de quebrazón y destrucción. Silencio. Luego se oye un largo alarido de* TERESA. *Pasan minutos. Silencio. Se oyen dos detonaciones desde el interior de la casa. Salen corriendo los atacantes. El primero en salir, descubierto, es el* CABALLERO TRAMPOSO, *que rápidamente se cubre con el capuchón. Galope de caballos que se alejan. Se enrojecen las ventanas. Comienza a salir humo de incendio de la casa de Murieta. Acuden* HOMBRES Y MUJERES *y el* VENDEDOR DE PÁJAROS, *quien lleva a la espalda una gran jaula con algunas palomas en el interior. Entran, sacan sillas y enseres precipitadamente. El incendio continúa. De pronto alguien grita.*)

Una voz—

La mataron!

Otra voz—

Es Teresa!

Otra voz—

Está muerta!

(*Las* MUJERES *se arrodillan, frente a la casa. Se oye un lamento musical que dura hasta el final de la escena. Los* HOMBRES *se agrupan junto al* VENDEDOR DE PÁJAROS. *Uno de ellos, recién salido de la casa, con algunos platos en la mano que deposita uno a uno junto al* PAJARERO, *dice, sin dirigirse a nadie y en voz baja*)

Hooded Men—

Is this the residence of Mr. Murieta, please, ma'm?

Voice of Teresa—

Joaquín isn't here. He left with the lavaderos this morning.
    He hasn't come back from the hills.

Hooded Men—

In that case, ma'm, we'll presoom on your hospitality. We'll
    come in and wait.

(*They hurl themselves on the door. It opens to their fists. They enter the
house. Noises. A sound of general wreckage.*)

Voice of Teresa—

Help! Dios mío! Socorro! Asesinos!

(*They all enter. The noise of ruthless pillage and destruction continues.
Then a silence. Later a long wail from* TERESA. *Minutes pass. Silence.
Then laughter. Two shots are heard from within. The attackers exit on the
run. The first to leave, unhooded now, is the* GENTLEMAN
SWINDLER, *who quickly covers up again with his hood. A sound of
receding hoofbeats . . . The windows redden; smoke pours from the
house of Murieta. Then* MEN *and* WOMEN *are seen rushing to the
rescue, including a* BIRD VENDOR *carrying a vertical stack of bird
cages on his back, with a few pigeons visible. They enter the house, pulling
out chairs and household chattels at top speed. Suddenly there is a piercing
cry.*)

Voice—

Ay-y-y! Dios mío! Asesinos! Ratones! Gringos malditos! They've
    murdered Teresa!

Others—

Sinvergüenzas! Hijos de perras! It's our little Teresa!

Un hombre—

La violaron también!

(Un murmullo de odio recorre el grupo.)

Voces—

Salvajes!

Voces—

Hay que avisarle a Joaquín!

Voces—

Hay que llamar a Murieta!

Vendedor de pájaros—

Compañeras palomas, vuelen a buscarlo! No vuelan sin él!

(Vuelan las palomas. Cierra la jaula vacía. Se seca las lágrimas con un pañuelo de colores. Sale lentamente entre las MUJERES ARRODILLADAS, *diciendo)*

Vendedor de pájaros—

Hasta cuándo!

Voz de mujeres—

Hasta cuándo!

(Largo silencio. Se oye un grito trágico en la voz de Murieta. Las mujeres, que estaban arrodilladas, se levantan súbitamente y hablan al unísono.)

Coro femenino—

Venganza es el hierro, la piedra, la lluvia, la furia, la lanza,
la llama, el rencor del destierro, la paz crepitante,

Voice—

She's dead! Joaquín's Teresita is dead!

(*The* W O M E N *kneel in front of the house. A wailing is heard throughout the remainder of the scene. The* M E N *cluster around the* B I R D V E N D O R. *One of them, just out of the house with some plates in his hand, stacks them one by one near the* B I R D V E N D O R, *and says more to himself than to the others, in a choked voice:*)

Man—

They raped her and left her for dead!

(*A wave of revulsion and hate runs through the group.*)

Voices—

Jackals! Hyenas! Culebras! Savages! Savages!

Voices—

Get word to Joaquín!

Voices—

We've got to find Murieta!

Bird Vendor—

Little playmates, little pigeons—find Murieta. Don't come
     back without him. Vamos, creaturas!

(*The pigeons fly off. He closes the empty bird cages. Then he dries his tears with a bandanna. He plods slowly toward the* K N E E L I N G W O M E N. *He speaks.*)

Bird Vendor—

How long? How long? How long?

Y el hombre distante enceguece clamando en la sombra
   venganza,
buscando en la noche esperanza sangrienta y castigo constante.
Despierta el huraño y recorre a caballo la tierra nocturna,
   Dios mío,
qué busca el oscuro al acecho del daño que brilla en su mano
   cortante?
Venganza es el nombre instantáneo de su escalofrío
que clava la carne o golpea en el cráneo o asusta con boca
   alarmante.
Y mata y se aleja el danzante mortal galopando a la orilla del
   río.

(*Se retira el* CORO FEMENINO, *salvo tres* SOLISTAS, *que escuchan
la* CANCIÓN MASCULINA *con la cabeza gacha.*)

Women's Voices—

How long, Dios mío, how long?

Women's Chorus—

Vengeance is all. Vengeance is mine, saith the Lord! Steel,
    stone, storm, rage, and the lance!
Out of the flame, the wrath of the dispossessed, the sinister
    dance!
Our men look out blindly, crying Revenge! in the distance and
    darkness,
prowling the night for redress, the hoped-for letting of blood.
And one taciturn man is aroused. He assaults the night and
    the land. He hurls his horse forward. Dios mío!
What does the Dark One carry in the ambush of danger that
    gleams in the fist of his fingers?
He carries revenge: its hairs stand on end, its chill
drives under his flesh, batters his brain. The voice of his terror
    is rampant.
Joaquín dances mortally on in the distance, scouring the
    beaches and rivers, and killing.

(WOMEN'S CHORUS *retires. Only three* SOLOISTS *remain to listen
to the* MEN'S SONG *which follows, their heads inclined.*)

CUADRO
QUINTO

EL FULGOR DE
JOAQUÍN

(En silueta aparecen ahorcados colgando de árboles y vigas.
CABALGATAS.)

Canción masculina—

Con el poncho embravecido
y el corazón destrozado,
galopa nuestro bandido
matando gringos malvados.

Por estas calles llegaron
estos hombres atrevidos,
se encontraron con Joaquín
y Joaquín con su destino.

Recitado—

*Ya
cayó uno,
ya van dos:
son siete,
lo digo yo.*

Galopa con poncho rojo
en su caballo con alas,

SCENE FIVE

THE SPLENDOR OF JOAQUÍN

(*The silhouettes of hanged men dangling from trees and beams. Then* HORSEMEN *in posses.*)

Men's Song—

His poncho bells in the air.
A Bandit gallops ahead,
in the night of his spirit's despair,
leaving the gringos for dead.

Those who ride on a dare,
the schemers lying in wait,
find Joaquín in his agony there:
and Joaquín finds his fate.

Recitative—

First one
and then one;
and then two,
till seven are gored by a gun:
and justice is done!

> Till his poncho is red
> and his horse rises on wings.

y allí donde pone el ojo,
mi vida, ay, pone la bala.

Y cómo se llama este hombre?
Joaquín Murieta es su nombre.

TRIO DE VOCES FEMENINAS

(*Acompañado por las voces de un* CORO INTERIOR *que está entre
telones. Al terminar la* CANCIÓN MASCULINA, *las tres* SOLISTAS
levantan la cabeza e interrogan al público.)

Solista 1—

Dónde está este jinete atrevido, vengando a su pueblo, a su
    raza, a su gente?

Solista 2—

Dónde está el solitario insurgente? Qué niebla ocultó su
    vestuario?

Solista 3—

Dónde están su caballo y su rayo, sus ojos ardientes?

Las tres—

Se encendió intermitente, en tinieblas acecha su frente.
Y en el día de las desventuras, recorre un corcel. La venganza
    va en esa montura.

Coro interior—

Galopa!

Solista 1—

"Galopa!" le dice la arena que tragó la sangre de los
    desdichados.

Joaquín fixes his eye, a bullet sings
out, and a gringo drops dead.

I speak for that lonely vendetta.
I call it by name: Joaquín Murieta.

TRIO OF WOMEN'S VOICES

(*Accompanied by an* UNSEEN CHORUS *behind-stage. At the
conclusion of the* MEN'S SONG, *the three* SOLOISTS *lift their heads
and address their questions directly at the audience.*)

Solo 1—

Where is that implacable Horseman, the Avenger in search of
   our birthright, our country, our race?

Solo 2—

Where is that lonely Insurgent? What cloud darkens his sullen
   apparel?

Solo 3—

Who has followed the flash of his eyes or his spurs, the hoofs
   or the glint on the gun barrel?

All Three—

His forehead looms big in the dark, his face is a flickering
bonfire. He rides in a dark time. Vengeance is cinched to his
   saddle.

Unseen Chorus—

There he gallops!

Solo 1—

"He gallops!" the sand says, soaked in the blood of the
   wretched.

Solista 3—

Y alguna chilena prepara un asado escondido para el forajido
que llega cubierto de polvo y de muerte.

Solista 2—

"Entrega esta flor al bandido y que tenga suerte."

Solista 3—

"Tú dale, si puedes, esta gallinita," susurra una vieja de Angol
de cabeza marchita.

Solista 2—

"Y tú, dale el rifle," dice otra, "de mi asesinado marido. Aún
está manchado con sangre de mi bienamado."

Solista 1—

Y este niño le da su juguete, un caballo de palo, y le dice:
"Jinete, galopa a vengar a mi hermano que un gringo mató
por la espalda."

Las tres—

Y Murieta levanta la mano y se aleja violento con el caballito
en las manos del viento.

Solista 3—

Y dice la madre:

Voz interior—

"Yo soy una espiga sin grano y sin oro,
no existe el tesoro que mi alma adoraba. Colgado en la viga,
mi Pedro, hijo mío, murió asesinado y lo lloro.
Y ahora, mis lágrimas Murieta ha secado con su valentía."

Solo 3—

"I see a woman in hiding. She brings meat newly roasted to
    comfort a Forager in his dust and his dying."

Solo 2—

"Place this flower in his hand to wish him Godspeed. Say that
    I pray for a Bandit."

Solo 3—

"Tell him we send him this capon," say the women of Angol,
    the withering mothers.

Solo 2—

"Give him this rifle," says another, "in the name of the
    youthfully dead. It cost me the blood of my lover."

Solo 1—

A child comes with a toy. He brings a straw horse, and he says:
    "Horseman, ride on. Ride in the name of my brother. He
    was shot in the back by a gringo."

All Three—

Murieta salutes them. He mounts his straw horse. He grows
    small in the wind and the distance, and is lost.

Solo 3—

A mother says:

Unseen Chorus—

"Wheat without kernel or gold was my lot.
The treasure that gave me my life is all spent.
My Pedro swung from a beam, cut down at the door.
Now I lament
with some profit. Murieta has settled the score."

Solista 2—

Y la otra, enlutada y bravía, mostrando el retrato de su
    hermano muerto,
levanta los brazos enhiestos, y besa la tierra que pisa el caballo
    de Joaquín Murieta.

Coro interior—

Galopa Murieta!

Las tres—

Galopa Murieta!

Solista 3—

La sangre caída decreta que un ser solitario
recoja en su ruta el honor del planeta.

Solista 1—

Y el sol solidario
despierta en la oscura llanura.

Solista 2—

Y la tierra sacude en los pasos errantes
de los que recuerdan amantes caídos y hermanos heridos.

Las tres—

Y por la pradera se extiende una extraña quimera, un fulgor: es
    la furia de la primavera,
y la amenazante alegría que lanza, porque cree que son una cosa
    victoria y venganza.

(*Se retiran las* SOLISTAS *por la izquierda. Entran* TRESDEDOS *y*
REYES *por la derecha.*)

Reyes—

Parece que se armó la grande! Usted que sabe más que yo de lo

Solo 2—

Another, enraged and bereaved, raises her arms their full
    length.
She shows a dead brother's picture; then kisses the earth
    touched by the horse of Joaquín, and wishes them
    strength.

Unseen Chorus—

Murieta is galloping!

All Three—

Murieta has passed!

Solo 3—

Blood is our witness. One lonely Rider hacks out a path to
    replenish our honor!

Solo 1—

One sun shines for us all and rises again on the dark of our
    planet!

Solo 2—

One continent, wracked by lost love and the wounding of
    brothers, takes new direction!

All Three—

Over the meadow arises the chimerical light of a Splendor:
    the fury of Spring in its strangeness,
the menacing joy that sees vengeance in victory and gains us
    our Penance!

(SOLOISTS *exit stage-left. Enter* THREE-FINGERS *and* REYES,
stage-right.)

que yo sé menos que usted, puede decirme qué vamos a
hacer ahora, compadre?

Tresdedos—

Con Murieta nos vamos! Hasta la muerte!

Reyes—

Hasta su muerte será, compadre! Por qué dispone de la mía?
Qué se la regaló mi mamita?

Tresdedos—

Allá en Copiapó lo aprendí, compadre! Cuando estalla el
barreno, la tierra tiembla, se oscurece el cielo y la piedra
dura se rompe en pedazos. No haga caso de la explosión, no
le haga caso al humo. Aquí está la piedra dura y hay que
romper la piedra o romperse el alma! . . . No ha visto
nuestros hermanos heridos? La sangre caída por todas
partes? Es nuestra sangre! Ya somos viejos, pero éste es
nuestro destino! Yo creo en la venganza, pues por ahí puede
comenzar la victoria.

(*Entra el* I N D I O.)

Tresdedos—

Alto! Quién va!

Indio—

Rosendo Juárez anda buscando al general Murieta.

Tresdedos—

Y quién es ese Rosendo Juárez?

Indio—

Rosendo Juárez soy yo.

Reyes—

It begins to look as though the whole coast is up in arms. You
seem to know so much more of what I understand less and
less. Maybe you can tell me what we do next, compadre?

Three-Fingers—

We sign up with Murieta, to the last man, my good buddy.
We follow him to the death!

Reyes—

To *your* death, you mean! Don't be so quick to give away
mine! My gray-haired old mother ain't giving away any
presents!

Three-F.—

I learned something once in Copiapó, my good buddy.
Whenever the big drills explode, the earth rattles your
teeth; a big cloud blackens the sun, and the solid rock
goes up like matchwood. You don't waste time worrying
which way the smoke went or where the next explosion is
coming from. It's the same here in California. The rock
all around us ain't gold: but it's solid! Either the rock
explodes or we do. Count up the dead and the wounded.
Blood flows all around us. Our blood! Mebbe we're not as
young as we used to be, but we know what needs to be
done. I believe in revenge because there's nothing else left,
compadre.

(*Enter an* INDIAN.)

Three-F.—

(*Stiffening.*)

Alto! Quíen va!

Tresdedos—

Qué quieres hablar con Murieta?

Indio—

Quiero pedirle que nos defienda.

Tresdedos—

Y qué les pasa a los indios?

Indio—

Lo que digo me sale del corazón y lo diré con una lengua
    derecha, porque el Gran Espíritu me mira y me oye. Estos
    gringos no dicen la verdad. Nos quitan el oro o se lo llevan
    en el juego. Los podemos echar y lo haremos con piedras,
    con arcos, con flechas. Dicen buenas palabras, pero éstas no
    sirven. Con palabras no se pagan los insultos ni los muertos.
    No sacan a mi padre de su tumba. Las palabras no pagan
    nuestras tierras, no pagan los caballos ni el ganado que nos
    quitan. Las buenas palabras no me devolverán mis hijos ni
    darán buena salud a mi gente. Todos los hombres fueron
    hechos por el mismo Gran Espíritu y si los gringos blancos
    quieren vivir en paz con los indios, pueden vivir en paz.
    Todos los hombres son hermanos y la tierra es la madre de
    todos. Pero la condición de mi gente me rompe el corazón
    y tenemos que pelear para protegernos. Rosendo Juárez ha
    terminado de hablar.*

Tresdedos—

Amigo Rosendo Juárez. Hay mucho que andar todavía. Pero ven
    con nosotros.

(A REYES)

---

* Este parlamento es transcripción textual de un documento publicado en
The Last of the California Rangers, de Jill L. Cossley-Batt.

Indian—

Rosendo Juárez. I've come to speak with the General, Murieta.

Three-F.—

And who might Rosendo Juárez be?

Indian—

Rosendo Juárez has come to speak with your General.

Three-F.—

Speak about what?

Indian—

I've come to ask him to stand up for us.

Three-F.—

Why? What's happening in Indian territory?

Indian—

I speak what I feel. I speak in plain language. I speak in the
   name of the Great Spirit who sees all that we do and
   knows all that we say. These gringos do not say the Thing
   That Is So. They rob all our gold or take it by treachery.
   We do what we can with bows and arrows, with stones,
   with our bare hands. All we get is fine words—no good to
   anyone. Words do not wipe out their insults or bring back
   the dead. Words do not rouse my dead father from the
   burial mound. Words do not pay for land wasted or the
   flocks and the herds taken by stealth. Fine words won't
   call back my sons or restore the health of my people. All
   men are one. The same Great Spirit created us all. If the
   white gringo wished to live peacefully with his Indian
   brother, he could do so. All men are brothers and the earth
   is mother of us all. The suffering of my people hits at my

No ve, compadre? Qué me dice ahora?

Reyes—

Sabe que me estoy convenciendo, compadre Tresdedos?

Tresdedos—

Así tenía que ser! Hemos sido hermanos en tantas desgracias.
Ahora nos vamos con Murieta! Apretarse los cinturones!
Joaquín! Joaquín!

(Se oye un silbido.)

Los tres—

Allá vamos!

(Entran tres H O M B R E S.*)*

Hombre 1—

Adónde van?

Tresdedos—

Esto no se aguanta más! Nos vamos con Murieta.

Hombre 2—

Queremos ir con ustedes!

Hombre 3—

Y yo también!

Coro de hombres—

Murieta! Murieta! Contigo, Murieta!

*(Una ráfaga de hombres invade el escenario. Los hombres se agrupan y
cantan al mismo tiempo que bailan una danza que mima escenas de
ferocidad y asalto.)*

heart. We must fight to protect ourselves now. Rosendo
Juárez has spoken.*

Three-F.—

Rosendo Juárez, we travel a long road and a lonely one. Come
travel with us, my friend.

(*To* REYES)

And you, Reyes, are you with us, too? Are your eyes open now?

Reyes—

Seen enough. Heard enough. I'm with you to the death,
Three-Fingers!

Three-F.—

There's no other way for us. Indian, Chilean, Mexican—
friends to the end, for better or worse. Saddle up. Let's
find Murieta . . . Joaquín! Joaquín Murieta!

(A *whistle is heard.*)

All Three—

Let's go.

(*Enter three* MEN.)

Man 1—

Where you off to?

Three-F.—

We're fed up. We're riding with Murieta.

* This speech is a textual transcription of a document published in *The
Last of the California Rangers,* by Jill L. Cossley-Batt. (Neruda's footnote)

Coro de los Asaltantes—

Llegaron las cuchilladas
    qué alegría,
aquí se matan por nada
    madre mía!

Aquí se juega y se canta
    y se maldice
y el pobre diablo que cae
    que agonice!

A nadie le importa un pito
lo que sucede en el cielo,
si me caigo de un balazo
no habré de pasar del suelo:
si me tienen que matar
del suelo no he de pasar!

Le voy a romper la crisma
al que me lance un sermón,
y a la rubia que me quiera
le comeré el corazón!

(Los A S A L T A N T E S *detienen su danza con un gesto amenazador hacia*
el público. Se oye una V O Z *desde dentro.*)

Una voz—

Aquí hay una sorpresa!

Un Asaltante—

Pasa la sorpresa!

Otro—

Pesa mucho?

Man 2—

We're riding with you.

Man 3—

Count me in, too.

Men's Chorus—

Murieta! Joaquín Murieta! Deal us in, Murieta.

(*Another wave of men invades the stage. They arrange themselves in groups. They sing, while dancing a dance which mimes motifs of attack and aggression.*)

Chorus of Attackers—

The long knives are here!
Holy Mother of us all,
they cut whatever they please. They fall
in, to the hilt: everywhere, anywhere.

It is time: time for the curse
and the song and the dangerous game.
Devil take all—all's one to us
now. We all bleed the same.

Whatever waits up in the sky,
I don't give a damn. Above
or below, we're already dead as they die!
If a bullet catches us on the move,
we'll shake off the dust of our birth
without digging a hole in the earth!

So help me, I'll clout
any guy who comes preaching a sermon!
Any whore of a gringa who opens her legs like a woman
will end with her heart eaten out!

Todos—

Es oro?

Otra voz—

Vale más que el oro! Allá va!

(*Entran dos* ASALTANTES *arrastrando al* CABALLERO
TRAMPOSO *y lo depositan en medio del escenario. Se ve inmensamente
alto, con los brazos abiertos. Parece un muñeco.*)

Los Asaltantes—

—Es el ladrón!
—Es el jefe de los Galgos!
—Es el asesino!
—Éste es el que me robó hasta mi ojo de vidrio!
—Bandido!
—Tú mataste a mi hermano!
—Tú incendiaste mi casa!
—Que lo pague todo ahora!

(*El* CABALLERO TRAMPOSO *trata de escaparse.*)

Tresdedos—

Atención! Apunten! Fuego!

(*Disparan. El* CABALLERO TRAMPOSO *cae al centro del escenario
como un monigote inerte.*)

Un Asaltante—

Y ahora, hacia Arroyo Cantova! A repartir el oro a los pobres.
    Allá nos esperan!

(*El* CORO DE LOS ASALTANTES *hace mutis mimando una cabalgata
mientras cantan la coda de "Llegaron las cuchilladas." Entran los*

(*The* ATTACKERS *end their dance with a menacing gesture toward the audience. A* VOICE *is heard offstage.*)

Voice—

Well, here's a nice surprise!

Attacker—

Screw your surprises!

Other—

How many carats?

All—

It's a bonanza!

Other—

All the gold in Sonora won't buy what we've got!

(*Enter two* ATTACKERS *dragging after them the* GENTLEMAN SWINDLER. *They dump him midstage. He suddenly seems enormously tall, like a doll or an idol, with wide-open arms.*)

Attackers—

—It's old Slippery Fingers himself!
—The Grand Wizard of the Brotherhood of Bloodhounds!
—Murderer!
—It's the son of a bitch who run off with my granddaddy's ticker!
—Maldito bandido!
—You shot my brother in the back, you white bastard!
—You burned down my house! He's come to collect on the mortgage!
—You'll get what you come for, with interest!

(*The* GENTLEMAN SWINDLER *tries to escape.*)

GALGOS *encapuchados y descubren el cuerpo inerte del* CABALLERO TRAMPOSO.)

Encapuchado primero—

Y éste, quién es?

Encapuchado segundo—

Es Él!

Encapuchado tercero—

Está muerto!

Encapuchado cuarto—

Está vivo!

Encapuchado primero—

Éste no muere nunca! Escúchanos! Puedes responder? Quiénes
   fueron?

Cab. Tramposo—

(*Con voz vacilante.*)

Los de Murieta. Se llevaron el oro! Mataron a todos los hombres.
   Acuchillaron a las mujeres.

(*Los* GALGOS *se yerguen lanzando un aullido rabioso y ejecutan una
grotesca danza ritual para revivir al* CABALLERO TRAMPOSO, *mientras
entonan un ensalmo.*)

Los Galgos—

Alfacadabra, Betacadabra, Blancocadabra!
Revive Trampón! Salta Saltón!
Blancocadabra, Betacadabra, Alfacadabra!
Salta Saltón! Revive Trampón!

Three-F.—

Nail him down good!

(*A volley of shots. The* GENTLEMAN SWINDLER *falls forward, center-stage, in one piece, like a puppet.*)

Attacker—

Now let's tell them at Arroyo Cantova! They can use some
    good news. They've sweated it out for these nuggets!

(*Exit* CHORUS OF ATTACKERS, *miming a posse in movement,
while they repeat the coda "The long knives are here." Enter the*
BLOODHOUNDS, *still hooded. They discover the inert figure of the*
GENTLEMAN SWINDLER.)

Bloodh. 1—

What the hell has happened?

Bloodh. 2—

It's the Grand Wizard himself!

Bloodh. 3—

He's dead! My God, he's dead!

Bloodh. 4—

No—he ain't! He's alive! There's no one can out-whiz the
    Grand Wizard!

Bloodh. 1—

Can you hear us? Can you tell us what's happened? Who did
    it? Who?

Gent. Swindler—

(*In a wavering voice*)

(Al final del ensalmo, los GALGOS *se prosternan y el* CABALLERO TRAMPOSO *emerge de un brinco y pronuncia la sentencia. Mientras corean la sentencia, los* GALGOS *se hacen más y más estridentes.)*

Cab. Tramposo—

Él debe morir!

Los Galgos—

Murieta debe morir!

Cab. Tramposo—

Nos roba lo que hemos robado con nuestros esfuerzos.

Los Galgos—

Murieta debe morir!

Cab. Tramposo—

Es un subversivo!

Los Galgos—

Murieta debe morir!

Cab. Tramposo—

Son indios! No entienden el progreso!

Los Galgos—

Murieta debe morir!

Cab. Tramposo—

Juremos aquí mismo su muerte!

Los Galgos—

Murieta debe morir!

It was Murieta's crowd. They took off with the gold. They
   murdered the men. Stabbed the women and children and
   took off with the gold.

(A *wild howl from the* B L O O D H O U N D S.)

Get Murieta!

All—

Get Murieta!

Gent. Swindler—

He robbed what we confiscated legal and proper!

All—

Get Murieta!

Gent. Swindler—

I pronounce him subversive!

All—

Get Murieta!

Gent. Swindler—

I pronounce them all Indians! I pronounce them a menace to
   Progress!

All—

Get Murieta!

Gent. Swindler—

Swear by the Sign of the Brotherhood! Swear by my death!
   Get Murieta!

All—

Get Murieta! Get Murieta! Get Murieta!

(Todos, ya de pie, levantan al cielo sus pistolones, disparan y se van apresuradamente.)

Coro femenino—

Adiós, compañero bandido. Se acerca la hora. Tu fin está claro y
    oscuro.
Se sabe que tú no conoces, como el meteoro, el camino seguro.
Se sabe que tú te desviaste en la cólera como un vendaval
    solitario.
Pero aquí te canto porque desgranaste el racimo de ira.
Y se acerca la aurora.
Se acerca la hora en que el iracundo no tenga ya sitio en el
    mundo.
Y una sombra secreta no habrá sido tu hazaña, Joaquín Murieta.

Voz del Poeta—

Pregunta el poeta: "No es digno este extraño soldado de luto
que los ultrajados le otorguen el fruto del padecimiento?"
No sé. Pero siento tan lejos aquel compatriota lejano,
que a través del tiempo merece mi canto y mi mano.
Porque defendió mostrando la cara, los puños, la frente,
la pobre alegría de la pobre gente saqueada por el invasor
    inclemente y amargo.
Y sale del largo letargo en la sombra un lucero
y el pueblo dormido despierta ligero siguiendo la huella escarlata
    de aquel guerrillero,
del hombre que mata y que muere siguiendo una estrella.
Por eso pregunta el poeta si alguna cantata requiere
aquel caballero bandido que dio al ofendido una rosa concreta:
justicia se llama la ira de mi compatriota Joaquín Murieta.

(All stand erect, raise their pistols and simultaneously fire into the air.
Then they rush offstage.)

Women's Chorus—

Adiós, compañero bandido! It is time. Your death lightens and
    darkens and comes nearer.
Yours never to know or to choose the path that lies open before
    you, sure as a meteor.
We see it all clearly. You veered in your rage as the hurricane
    veers in a void.
You die opportunely. You threshed fine the grain of your anger.
    We sing
of a morning approaching,
of the hour when a man's indignation, grown larger than life,
    surpasses all stigma.
All that you did is known to us now, Joaquín Murieta. We
    speak the enigma.

Poet's Voice—

But a Poet may ask: "What can be said for this Stranger, this
    Soldier, this Mourner,
to whom a time's outrage brought only a harvest of havoc?"
I say: time does not divide us: I feel the abuse of my
    countryman,
however lost or removed. He merits my song and my art.
He welcomed all hazard: gave his face and his fists and his
    heart to defend
the humble pursuits of the landless, the little joys left by a
    heartless invader.
He brought light to the dark of the endless ordeal of their
    lethargy.
A sleeping nation awoke to its need on the reddening path of
    this soldier:
the murderer who murdered the murderers and died for our
    honor.

A poet considered the right and the wrong of this Bandit's
   Cantata:
the Song of a Gentleman Outlaw who offered his best, the rose
   of his death, to the neediest.
I call the rage of my countryman just, and I sing of Joaquín
   Murieta.

C U A D R O
S E X T O

—

MUERTE DE MURIETA

(*La escena se oscurece totalmente. Silencio. En la oscuridad una cara blanca de* MUJER, *como de tiza, con manto chileno, aparece. Sólo se ve su rostro. Dice el casi soneto, mientras el* CORO *permanece inmóvil en la penumbra.*)

CASI SONETO

Pero, ay, aquella tarde lo mataron:
fue a dejar flores a su esposa muerta,
y de pronto el heroico acorralado
vio que la vida le cerró la puerta.

De cada nicho un yanqui disparaba,
la sangre resbalaba por sus brazos
y cuando cien cobardes dispararon,
un valiente cayó con cien balazos.

Y cayó entre las tumbas desgranado
allí donde su amor asesinado,
su esposa, lo llamaba todavía.

Su sangre vengadora y verdadera

SCENE
SIX

DEATH OF MURIETA

(The stage in total darkness. Silence. Out of the darkness materializes the white face of a W O M A N—*chalk-white, wearing a scarf in the Chilean style. Only her face is visible. She speaks the Almost Sonnet, while the* C H O R U S *remains motionless in the shadows.)*

ALMOST SONNET

And that evening they killed him—woe to the murderer!
He came with fresh flowers for the grave of his wife
and felt himself circled like sheep in the noose of the herder.
A door slammed on the heroic heart of that life.

From every direction, gringos with guns. They all opened fire.
His body broke open, blood drained from his arms. He reared
like a stallion as a hundred shots toppled him there
and a hundred cowards, coming out of their corners,
    fired.

He slumped over the gravestones scattered like seed
on the withering mounds where the wraith of Teresa
called to her husband from the sleep of the tomb.

Then his vengeance discovered its implacable need:

pudo besar así a su compañera
y ardió el amor allí donde moría.

(*Estalla la música de la muerte. El* CORO *se repliega al fondo formando
un friso funerario a ambos lados de una tumba humilde. Al mismo
tiempo, y sobre el ritmo agitado de la música obsesionante, irrumpen en
el escenario seis* GALGOS *que ejecutan una danza frenética. Esta
danza representa la acción de una jauría de perros ladrando, aullando,
olfateando por todos los rincones en busca de una presa. Dan la impresión
de que llevan un arma con la cual apuntan a cada rincón que les parece
sospechoso. Ritmo demoníaco y atmósfera de ferocidad monstruosa. El
cuarteto de* SOLISTAS, *que se han desprendido del* CORO, *colocándose
a ambos lados de la boca del escenario, expresan, durante la danza,
advertencias a Murieta, esforzándose para que sus voces sobresalgan por
encima del tumulto de la música y el baile.*)

(*Inmediatamente después del estampido inicial.*)

Solista 1—

Escucha la arena
que mueve el desierto!

Solista 2—

Escucha el reloj
que entierra a los muertos!

Solista 3—

Atrás, bandolero!
La muerte te aguarda!

Solista 4—

Llegaron los Galgos!

Solista 1—

Murió una guitarra!

to kiss with his blood and his body his companion and play
  fellow,
till love blazed its last and lighted them both to their doom.

(The Death Music explodes, at this point. The CHORUS *realigns itself
backstage, forming a funeral frieze on both sides of the modest grave. At
the same time, over the agitated rhythms of obsessional music, six*
BLOODHOUNDS *leap onstage and begin a frenetical dance. The dance
suggests the behavior of a cageful of barking dogs, howling, sniffing into
every corner in pursuit of their quarry. They give the impression that they
are armed, with weapons that they aim into every suspicious nook. A
demoniacal rhythm and an atmosphere of monstrous ferocity. The quartet
of* SOLOISTS *disengage themselves from the* CHORUS, *arranging
themselves on either side of the stage apron, punctuate the dance with
their allusion to* MURIETA, *forcing their voices to surmount the tumult
of music and dance.)*

(Immediately after the opening barrage.)

Solo 1—

Listen to the sand
moving the desert!

Solo 2—

Listen to the clock
burying the dead!

Solo 3—

Bandolero, stand back!
Death watches you, one step ahead!

Solo 4—

The Hounds beat the bushes.

Solo 1—

A guitar breaks its string.

Solista 2—

Tu sangre invisible
será derramada!

Solista 3—

Oíste, Murieta?

Solista 4—

La tierra te advierte!

Solistas 1 y 2—

Se cumple el destino!

Solista 4—

Los galgos te acechan!

Solista 3—

Termina tu suerte!

Solista 1—

Te siguen las huellas!

Solista 2—

Por ese camino
se acerca la muerte!

Solista 4—

No traigas la rosa
para tu Teresa!

Los cuatro solistas—

Te aguarda la fosa!

Solista 3—

Teresa dormía.

Solo 2—

Your blood, from its underground veins,
is spilled like a spring.

Solo 3—

Do you hear, Murieta?

Solo 4—

Do you hear the hue and cry of the rock?

Solos 1, 2—

It says that your end is accomplished.

Solo 4—

The Bloodhounds are poised in the blinds.

Solo 3—

Your clock has run down. This is the last of your luck.

Solo 1—

The dogs have nosed out your track.

Solo 2—

Death closes in
from behind.

Solo 4—

Never mind
the red rose for Teresa!

All Four—

Beware of the ditch!

Solo 3—

Teresa sleeps soundly.

Solista 1—

Por qué despertarla?

Solistas 2 y 4—

Para qué regar
con sangre su cara?

Los cuatro solistas—

Murieta, detente!

Solista 4—

Separa tus pasos!

Solista 3—

La rosa que llevas, separa!

Solista 2—

Caerán tus ojos!

Solista 1—

Y se pudrirá tu mirada!
Tus brazos serán una cruz derribada!

Solista 3—

Ya no montarás!

Solistas 3 y 4—

Ya no correrás!

Solistas 1, 3 y 4—

Ya no comerás!

Los cuatro solistas—

Ya no vengarás!

Solo 1—

Nothing will summon her back!

Solos 2, 4—

Why water the flower of that face
with your blood?

All Four—

Stand back, it will come to no good!

Solo 4—

Give your footsteps no space!

Solo 3—

Leave no trace of your roses!

Solo 2—

Seal your eyes shut!

Solo 1—

Your face has already rotted away!
Your arms are crossed sticks on a grave.

Solo 3—

You will never leap back to the saddle!

Solos 1, 3, 4—

You will never race on like a wave!

Solos 2, 4—

You will never take strength from your food!

All Four—

Forgive us!

Solista 1—

Ya no vivirás!

Solista 2—

Los galgos ya pisan
tus propias pisadas!

Solistas 1 y 4—

El frío del cielo
toca sus campanas!

Solista 3—

El llanto en la luna
la lluvia prepara!

Solistas 1, 2 y 4—

No te necesita
Teresa, que vive en tu alma!

Solista 3—

Arroja la rosa
que lleva tu mano malvada!

Solista 1—

Por qué tanta sangre?

Los cuatro solistas—

Quién es?

(*Súbitamente la danza se detiene y los* S O L I S T A S *se callan. Un haz de
luz cae en el centro del escenario y avanza hacia la tumba, que está al
fondo. Cuando la luz toca la tumba, los* G A L G O S, *agazapados en los
rincones, disparan. La luz se torna roja y una flor se abre sobre la tumba
de Teresa. Los cuatro* S O L I S T A S, *cubriéndose el rostro con un crespón
negro, gritan. La música vuelve violentamente. Los* G A L G O S *se*

You will never save or avenge us!
You will never outlive us!

Solo 2—

The Bloodhounds spade
down the tracks you have made.

Solos 1, 4—

In the cold of the noon
a bell tolls for you now.

Solo 3—

Grief readies the rain
in the moon for you now.

Solos 1, 2, 4—

Teresa lives in your soul:
how else can she serve you?

Solo 3—

Throw the dangerous rose
from your hand: let nothing unnerve you!

Solo 1—

We say there shall be no more blood!

(*A pause.*)

All Four—

What thing comes this way?

(*Suddenly the dance halts and the* SOLOISTS *are silent. A ray of light
falls center-stage and moves toward the grave, at the back. Then the light
touches the grave. The* BLOODHOUNDS, *crouched in the corners, fire
a volley of shots into it. The light turns red and a flower opens over the
grave of Teresa. The four* SOLOISTS, *covering their faces with black*

abalanzan sobre la tumba y, por breves segundos, miman ritmicamente
la acción de segar o de cortar algo a hachazos. Luego, se retiran. Cesa la
música. La flor ha desaparecido. El C O R O F E M E N I N O *avanza a*
primer plano para decir el lamento.)

LAMENTO

(Recitado por el C O R O F E M E N I N O.)

Se fue besando la tierra
donde dormía su esposa:
desarmado lo mataron.
Llevaba sólo una rosa
para Teresa, la muerta.
Se multiplicó la flor
con sus heridas abiertas
y dejó llena de rosas
la tumba de su Teresa.
Con una rosa en la mano
ha muerto Joaquín Murieta.
Murió como muere un rayo
y cayó junto a su muerta.
Tanto miedo le tenían
que se acercaban apenas
y disparaban aún
al cadáver de Murieta.
Y cuando ya se atrevieron,
para que no resucite,
le cortaron la cabeza
al muerto, en el cementerio.
Le cortaron la cabeza.
Al guerrillero caído,
le cortaron la cabeza.
Cuando ya no respiraba,
le cortaron la cabeza.

crepe, cry out. The music grows violent. The BLOODHOUNDS *tilt themselves over the grave for a few brief moments, rhythmically miming the action of scything and hacking down with an ax. Then they withdraw. The music stops. The flower disappears. The* WOMEN'S CHORUS *advances to the stage level to speak the Lament.)*

LAMENT

(*Recited by the* WOMEN'S CHORUS)

He was kissing the ground
where Teresa lay sleeping
when they shot him, unarmed.
He left what he could: a rose
for Teresa, with his blood and his blows.
Then one flower became legion:
all his wounds opened wide
and reddened the earth with the last of their roses
for the breast of his bride.

So great was the dread of the crowd
when the gunmen drew closer
with their rifles at ready
that they fired into the wounds of his body.
Then, when the death throes were over
and the breath had gone out of the body,
they laid violent hands on the dead
in the crosses and mounds of the cemetery,
and cut off his head.

Ay! they cut off his head!
When his courage could touch them no more
and he fell undefended
they struck with the weight of their axes
and cut off his head!

Tanto miedo le tenían
al bravo Joaquín Murieta,
que cuando murió el valiente
y no tenía defensa,
del miedo que le tenían,
le cortaron la cabeza.

(*Redoble de tambor y corneta de circo pobre. El* C O R O *se divide en
dos, colocándose a ambos lados del escenario. Aparece una barraca de feria
dividida en dos espacios por una cortina. En uno el* B A R R A Q U E R O,
que es el mismo C A B A L L E R O T R A M P O S O, *invita a los transeúntes.
En el otro está la* C A B E Z A D E M U R I E T A *en una jaula. La cabeza es
más grande que en el tamaño natural y tiene hilos de gotas de sangre, como
rosarios, que llegan al suelo. Los ojos abiertos. Durante la escena entrarán
incesantemente los mismos visitantes que darán la vuelta poniéndose
sombreros, mantas, bufandas diferentes, o bien, cambiando lo que
transportan, canastos, paraguas, niños en brazos, etc.*)

El Barraquero—

(*A gritos.*)

Entrad here a my barraca
for only twenty centavos.
Here is Joaquín Murieta,
aquí está el tigro encerrado.

       Freedom, freedom y negocios
       sólo por twenty centavos;
       única oportunidad,
       Murieta decapitado.

Here. Here veinte cents,
twenty centavos, señores,
una cabeza de tigro
en una jaula encerrado.

(Fanfare of bugles and drums, in the style of the Circus Fandango. The CHORUS *divides in two sections aligned on either side of the stage. A circus wagon, divided in two by a curtain, appears. In one section, a* BARKER—*none other than the* GENTLEMAN SWINDLER *himself—makes his pitch to the passers-by. In the other is the* HEAD OF MURIETA, *in a great cage. The* HEAD *is much larger than life, and is covered with blood-colored droplets and threads, like rosaries reaching to the ground. The eyes are wide-open, Byzantine. During the scene, people are constantly moving by, doffing and donning their hats, arranging their scarves, mufflers, in various shapes and lengths, or shifting whatever they carry in their arms—baskets, umbrellas, babies.)*

Barker—

(At the top of his voice)

Entrad here in mi barraca
for the trifling sum of twenty cents. See
the genuine Murieta,
the Tiger in captivity!

> Take your time! It's yours for free:
> a few centavos, Ladies and Gents!
> Here's your opportunity
> to see a head without the trimmin'!

This way, folks! For veinte cents,
twenty centavos—a modest figger!
Not to keep you in suspense—
see the Head without the Tiger!

Yours for veinte cents, señor!
Veinte coppers and no more!

> A Bandit's Head, clean
> as a cabbage, a bargain, Gents,

Señores, por veinte cents,
sólo por veinte centavos.

> La cabeza de Murieta
> por fin se la hemos cortado:
> qué barato twenty cents,
> entren a ver el malvado
> que tanto nos asustaba
> sólo por twenty centavos.

(*Estribillo.*)

> Freedom, freedom, etc.

(*Avanzan las* M U J E R E S *en actitud de increpar al público. Al promediar esta escena, ya se está desarrollando en la platea. Al terminar, las* M U J E R E S *salen corriendo hacia el foyer.*)

CORO FEMENINO

Todas—

Cómo dejan en la jaula,
como dejan
en la jaula del oprobio
su cabeza?

Una—

No recuerdan que sus manos
vengaron tantas ofensas?

Otra—

Y tiene abiertos los ojos
y cortada la cabeza?

Otra—

Porque sufrimos salió

at twenty cents—
the last, original Desperado!
a hunter's Bounty!
The Scourge of Calaveras County!

(*The* W O M E N *advance in an attitude of outraged rebuke. Dividing the stage in two, the action now spills into the orchestra pit. At its conclusion, the* W O M E N *exit toward the foyer, at a run.*)

WOMEN'S CHORUS

All—

How can you bear
to see that Head
caged in ignominy there,
vandalized and left for dead:
how do you dare!

One—

So little time
to have forgotten
hands that reddened for our crime?

All—

How do you dare!

Others—

For our great suffering and dearth
he cleansed a violated earth,
and died!

Others—

Have you blood to warm your veins?

Others—

Have you wit to light your spirit?

a galopar en la arena
y por nosotros mató.

Otra—

No tienen sangre en las venas?

Otra—

No tienen luz en el alma,

Otra—

no tienen manos chilenas,

Otra—

no tienen pies los zapatos.

Otra—

No has visto con qué tristeza
te mira el decapitado
buscándote y no te encuentra?

Todas—

Hay que robar a los gringos
su desdichada cabeza.

Otra—

Hay que darle sepultura
en la tumba de Teresa.

Otra—

Ella murió asesinada
y él por vengar su belleza,
llegó a tanta desventura!

Todas—

Hay que robar su cabeza!

Others—

Can Chile clench its fist again?

Others—

Shoeless once, can you endure it?

Others—

Have you no heart for the long sorrow
of those decapitated eyes
that gaze toward us and our tomorrow?

All—

Shame the gringo desecrator!
Restore that violated body!
Return him whole to his Creator!

All—

The Head! The Head of Murieta!

Others—

How infamous that separation!
All that pride of name and station,
the posture of his pure vocation
debased to this by shame and anguish!

All—

A barker's public exhibition!
The horror of it! Madre mía!
Abomination! Abomination!

Restore you hearts! Restore that Head!

MEN'S CHORUS

(*The* MEN *recapitulate the action mimed by the* WOMEN.)

Otra—

Qué infamia que en esa pieza
su condición orgullosa,
su apostura, su nobleza
derrotada y dolorosa!

Todas—

Todo eso en exhibición!

Otra—

Madre mía, qué vileza!

Unas—

Que no tienen corazón?

Todas—

Hay que robar la cabeza!

CORO VIRIL

(*Los* HOMBRES *repiten la acción realizada por las* MUJERES.)

Todos—

Qué esperamos los hombres, qué esperamos?
Tenemos corazón! Tenemos manos!

Uno—

Yo soy de La Serena y lo que tuve,
un puñado de oro, fue una nube.
No tengo qué perder sino las penas.
Padre y madre y mujer en La Serena
no los veré ya más. Cuenten conmigo.
El finado Joaquín era mi amigo.

All—

What does a man wait for? What moves a man? Start
with the strength of his hands! Start with his heart!

One—

I come from La Serena. I plowed
a fistful of gold. It has melted away like a cloud.
I've nothing to lose. I was never a winner.
Father, mother, and wife—all I had in Serena—
will never see me again. Count me in, to the end!
Joaquín Murieta is dead. Joaquín was my friend.

Another—

I hail from Loncomilla: the school of hard knocks.
I'm a man without roots or connections. I live like a river.
I go where Joaquín calls me: wherever, however, whenever.
Now his voice calls from the bars of a mountebank's box.

Another—

I lived like a stand of green corn in the spring.
I heard the rain fall on the wood. That's a good thing.
I kiss every stone of my land—but see where I've come!
To think that my bones will be buried this long way from home!
I was always a good man with keys. I can handle the locks.
Smash the mountebank's wagon to bits and break open his box!

Others—

Men of Talagante and Cherquenco,
men of Lebu, Rancagua, Quillota,
men of Púa, Taltal, Nacimiento,
Parral and Victoria: countrymen
of Tongoy, Renaico, Perquenco—
to the wagon! Break
axle, carriage, stave, and rafter!

Otro—

De Loncomilla soy, de los bravíos,
a mi nadie me ataja, soy un río,
y con Murieta voy donde me llame:
oigo su voz desde la jaula infame.

Otro—

Yo soy chilote y en la primavera
oigo caer la lluvia en la madera.
Mi tierra, me la comería a besos!
Pensar que aquí voy a dejar los huesos!
Yo abriré la barraca del malvado,
a mí no me resisten los candados.

Otro—

Hombres de Talagante o de Cherquenco,
de Lebu, de Rancagua, de Quillota,
de Púa, de Taltal, de Nacimiento,
de Parral, de Victoria, compatriotas
de Tongoy, de Renaico, de Perquenco,
a romper la barraca
y a romper
los huesos de ese mercader!

Unos—

A robar
la cabeza del capitán!

Otros—

Y aunque murió sin confesión,
a enterrarlo en su religión

Todos—

para que duerma con su espada
junto a su muerta bienamada.

Break the Box of the Zoo
and the bones of the Zoo Master!

Others—

And then, though he died without priest or confession,
give him the rites of his cult and religion!

All—

Side by side with the dust of his dearly adored,
lay him to rest with the cross of his sword!

(*Two* W O M E N, *backstage, place flowers on a grave and can be heard
praying in low voices. The* C O R T E G E *enters from backstage, moving
steadily forward, led by* T H R E E-F I N G E R S *and* R E Y E S, *who carry the*
H E A D   O F   M U R I E T A. *All walk in silence. The only thing that can be
heard is a tolling of bells that punctuates the* F U N E R A L   C H O R U S. *As
the* C O R T E G E *approaches the audience, the* P R A Y I N G   W O M E N *rise
to their feet, leaving the grave of Teresa in full view. During the
procession, the* F U N E R A L   C H O R U S *is heard.*)

Funeral Chorus—

The gold takes back its own: this funereal Mourner in the dust
        and the gold,
the Beheaded One, Soldier without crucifix, banner, or sun,
bloody and bled of his gold and terrestrial fury,
poor, violent, wandering man that sought the Mirage
of a ruinous light, a golden obsession,
trapped in the maze of his rancor and greed!
My Countryman, wounded and wrenched and nocturnal,
soldier of lonely misfortune,
exiled from the springtime of Chile, the replenishing joys he
        defended,
assaulting the moonlight,
determined and headstrong, unleashing the lightning of winter!
Murieta is dead in his pride—bandit or savior—what matter?

(Dos MUJERES, *al fondo del escenario, ponen flores en una tumba y rezan en voz baja. Entra el* CORTEJO *por el fondo de la sala y avanza hacia el escenario, encabezado por* TRESDEDOS Y REYES, *que llevan la* CABEZA DE MURIETA. *Todos marchan en silencio. Sólo se oye un redoble de campana puntuando el* CORO FUNERARIO. *Mientras el* CORTEJO *avanza entre el público, las* MUJERES *que oran en el escenario se levantan dejando en descubierto la tumba de Teresa. El cortejo llega hasta allí. Durante el desfile se oye el siguiente* CORO FUNERARIO.)*

Coro funerario—

El oro recibe a este muerto de pólvora y oro enlutado,
el descabellado, el chileno sin cruz de soldado, ni sol ni
    estandarte,
el hijo sangriento y sangrante del oro y la furia terrestre,
el pobre violento y errante que en la California dorada
siguió alucinante una luz desdichada: el oro su leche nutricia
le dio, con la vida y la muerte, acechado y vencido por odio y
    codicia.
Nocturno chileno arrastrado y herido por las circunstancias del
    daño incesante,
el pobre soldado y amante sin la compañera ni la compañía,
sin la primavera de Chile lejano ni las alegrías que amamos y
    que él defendía,
en forma importuna atacando en su oscuro caballo a la luz de la
    luna,
certero y seguro, este rayo de enero vengaba a los suyos.
Y muerto en su orgullo, si fue un bandolero no sé ni me importa.
    Ha llegado la hora
de una gran aurora que todas las sombras sepulta y oculta con
    manos de rosa fragante,
la hora, el minuto en que hallamos la eterna dulzura del mundo
    y buscamos
en la desventura el amor que sostiene la cúpula de la primavera.

We sing only the morning's ascension, hands hiding roses,
the minute and hour when the Seeker under the seed finds what
        he sought:
the honeycomb of the world in midst of misfortune, love lifting
        the spring like a cupola.
He fought under no banner. No colors saved him. He went
        down with the killers and losers,
a stranger turned gunman. Pity his shadow! We bring him a rose
from Teresa to atone for the blood that flows the world over,
· to roll back the stone on the cave of our violence and redeem
the heart's probity—lift it high as the wheat in the tassel, till
        gold is no longer
the sign of our wrath and our turpitude, and the bread that we
        wring from the earth
stings with war's aftertaste, the savor of bloody men fallen, no
        more!

(*Scene: A cemetery. Moonlight. Diggers prepare to dispose of the dead.
Several* PRAYING WOMEN. *The* HEAD OF MURIETA *speaks
from its mound: the* GRAVEDIGGERS *freeze in their places. The*
VAGABOND MUSICIAN *accompanies the monologue with a barely
audible melody. The sound of the wind blowing over the prairies.*)

The Head of Murieta Speaks—

With no one to hear me, I can whisper the truth, in the end:
a child has died in the shadows, a boy in the dark.
He will never know what demanded his death, he will not
        understand
why he moves through a wilderness now, without motive or
        mark.

After such loving—so great desolation!
After such fighting, so hard a defeat! I do not understand it.
I deliver myself to the hands of Teresa: the head of a bandit
sleeps in the lap of his love, and learns patience.

Y Joaquín Murieta no tuvo bandera sino sólo un dolor asesino.
    Y aquel desdichado
halló asesinado su amor por enmascarados. Y así un extranjero
    que salió a vencer y vivir
en las manos del oro, se tornó bandolero y llegó a padecer, a
    matar y morir.
Piedad a su sombra! Entreguemos la rosa que llevaba a su amada
    dormida,
a todo el amor y al dolor y a la sangre vertida, y en las puertas
    del odio esperemos
que regrese a su cueva la oscura violencia, y que suba la clara
    conciencia
a la altura madura del trigo y el oro no sea testigo de crimen y
    furia y el pan de mañana en la tierra
no tenga el sabor de la sangre del hombre caído en la guerra.

(*Escena en el cementerio. La luna. Cavan para enterrar el despojo. Algunas*
MUJERES *rezan. Habla la* CABEZA DE MURIETA. *Los*
ENTERRADORES *se* inmovilizan. *El* MÚSICO VAGABUNDO
acompaña el monólogo con una melodía que apenas se oye. Hay un ruido
de viento que silba en la llanura.)

Habla la Cabeza de Murieta—

Nadie me escucha, puedo hablar por fin,
un niño en las tinieblas es un muerto.
No sé por qué tenía que morir
para seguir sin rumbo en el desierto.

De tanto amar llegué a tanta tristeza,
de tanto combatir fui destruido
y ahora entre las manos de Teresa
dormirá la cabeza de un bandido.

Fue mi cuerpo primero separado,
degollado después de haber caído,

First they smashed through my body; then that vile separation—
the head shorn from the shoulders, my head in the dust.
Now the crime does not touch me; the smart of a man's
        defamation
is as nothing compared to the pang of the love that I lost.

Death was always lying in wait; and we met
on the hard road I traveled—an untimely encounter,
but one of my making: a lifetime's obsession with killing
and dying that brought us together at last, like paths at a gate.

I speak as a Head bled of its force and inflection.
The voice that I summon is strange; the lips are not mine.
What can the Dead say? the Dead with no other direction
than that which the wind takes as it works in the void of the
    rain?

To whom is it given to know? What intruder
or friend, tracing the naked truth in the snow,
shall interpret my story or sing it in truth, in the end?
My time is a hundred years hence. My lips shall be Pablo
        Neruda.

Not for the evil I did, or the evil others have done,
not for the little good fortune that lightened my strife,
but for some other cause that inheres in the dignity won
by the losers who forfeit the total intent of their life.

I say spring is unbreakable. Time has its way with the living.
Let the passing of time illumine my life, if it must,
not to sweeten its rancors, but to temper the just and unjust—
whatever advantage or loss remains for the taking or giving.

For all of life, all its lost evanescence,
is only a trick of our dreaming dismay, in the end—

no clamo por el crimen consumado,
sólo reclamo por mi amor perdido.

Mi muerta me esperaba y he llegado
por el camino duro que he seguido
a juntarme con ella en el estado
que matando y muriendo he conseguido.

Soy sólo una cabeza desangrada,
no se mueven mis labios con mi acento,
los muertos no debían decir nada
sino a través de la lluvia y el viento.

Pero cómo sabrán los venideros,
entre la niebla, la verdad desnuda?
De aquí a cien años, pido, compañeros,
que cante para mí Pablo Neruda.

No por el mal que haya o no haya hecho,
ni por el bien, tampoco, que sostuve,
sino porque el honor fue mi derecho
cuando perdí lo único que tuve.

Y así en la inquebrantable primavera
pasará el tiempo y se sabrá mi vida,
no por amarga menos justiciera
no la doy por ganada ni perdida.

Y como toda vida pasajera
fue tal vez con un sueño confundida.
Los violentos mataron mi quimera
y por herencia dejo mis heridas.

(*Cuando deja de hablar la* C A B E Z A *se mueven los* A C T O R E S. R E Y E S

both the men who laid violent hands on my lifetime's
    obsessions,
and the gift of my wounds I entrust to the love of a friend.

(When the H E A D ceases to speak, the O T H E R S begin to move again.
R E Y E S and T H R E E - F I N G E R S remain near the newly dug grave.
Silence. Then the F I N A L C H O R U S.)

Chanting Chorus—

Light breaks on the night of our vanished bereavement.
Now nothing is dark—not the night or the man or the spirit.
Out of revenge's impurity is born the dream of the spirit's
    achievement:
however immense our deprival, at length our detractors will hear
    it.

We wait without trembling or fear. Man's freedom is not
    preempted forever.
The color that darkens the language and skin of my country, all
    that a nation espouses,
will be honored. The Bloodhounds will sicken on the very
    hearth of their houses.

(Organ music, but muted. The V O I C E O F T H E P O E T takes over.)

Voice of the Poet—

Murieta, willful and violent child, return with my song to the
    metal and mines of your Chile.
All oaths are dissolved, your compass of vengeance comes full
    circle.
Your land has forgotten you now—the terror you wrought, the
    poor head under the sickle
are shadows that darken a dream. You were one of your
    country's romantics.

y TRESDEDOS *quedan junto a la tumba recién cavada. En el silencio,* *el* CORO FINAL.)

Coro cantado—

(Acompañado de órgano.)

La luz ilumina la noche de la desventura.
Y ya no es oscura la noche ni el alma del hombre es oscura.
Así, de la impura venganza, nació la segura esperanza.
Y si nuestra desdicha fue inmensa, más tarde tuvimos defensa.

No tendremos temor ni terror. No será derrotado el honor.
Serán respetados por fin el color de la piel y el idioma español.
Por fin encontraron castigo los Galgos en su propia casa.

(Sigue el órgano en sordina, mientras la VOZ DEL POETA *dice)*

Voz del Poeta—

Murieta, violento y rebelde, regresa en mi canto al metal y a las
    minas de Chile.
Ya su juramento termina entre tanta venganza cumplida.
La patria olvidó aquel espanto y su pobre cabeza cortada y caída
es sólo la sombra del sueño distante y errante que fue su
    romántica vida.

No es mío el reproche por su cabalgata de fuego y espanto.
Quién puede juzgar su quebranto: fue un hombre valiente y
    perdido.
Y para estas almas no existe un camino elegido:
El fuego lo lleva en sus dientes, los quema, los alza, los vuelve a
    su nido.
Y se sostuvieron volando en la llama: su fuego los ha consumido.

Regresa y descansa y galopa en el aire hacia el sur su caballo
    escarlata.

Not mine to censure the outcome: a cavalcade fearful and fiery;
or construe its destruction. I only know a brave man went under.
For spirits like yours, no path leads back to an option. They
    blunder,
their teeth grating fire, they burn, they rise like a phoenix, then
    return to their faraway aerie.
They take life from the coals that consume them; the coal burns
    them back to a cinder.

Joaquín, return to your nest: gallop the air toward the south on
    your blood-colored stallion.
The streams of the country that bore you sing out of silvery
    mouths. Your Poet sings with them.
Your fate mingled bloodshed and gall, Joaquín Murieta; but its
    sound
is still heard. Your people repeat both your song and your grief,
    like a tolling bell struck underground. The people are
    million.

(REYES and THREE-FINGERS stand at attention, holding out their
vertical rifles without raising them from the ground. Their faces are
resolute and somber.)

(Curtain)

Los ríos natales le cantan con boca de plata. Y le canta también
   el poeta.
Fue amargo y violento el destino de Joaquín Murieta. Desde este
   minuto
el Pueblo repite como una campana enterrada, mi larga cantata
   de luto.

Coro cantado—

(*Retoma el himno anterior in crescendo, hasta el máximo.*)

Oh, tú, Justiciero que nos amparaste, recibe las gracias de tus
   compañeros!
Alabado sea, que sea alabado tu nombre, Murieta!

(REYES *y* TRESDEDOS *se ponen en actitud de "firmes," adelantando
en un gesto los dos rifles verticales, sin levantarlos del suelo. Sus rostros
demuestran decisión y solemnidad.*)

APPENDICES

Why Joaquín Murieta?

I wrote a big book of poems . . . I called it *The Barcarole* . . .
a kind of ballad . . . I nibbled a bit of this and a bit of that out
of my stock of poetic staples—here a little water and wheat,
there a little ordinary sand, the hard outline of cliffs and quarries
. . . and the sea, of course, with its calms and its thunderclaps,
the eternities I watch over, here at my window, and bring to
order on paper . . . and in this book there are episodes that
sing and tell stories . . . That's how I do things . . . from the
very beginning . . . I can't manage otherwise . . . Well, one
day I picked and I prodded, a great cloud of dust arose like the
tail end of an earthquake, flying around till it turned into an
episode about a horse and its rider and started to gallop about in
my verses—very long verses, this time, like highways or
thoroughfares—and I rode herd behind them, verses and all, and
struck gold, California gold with Chileans panning the sand and
schooners under a full load of canvas sailing out of Valparaíso
. . . the greed and the turbulence of men, fundamental things
. . . this vendetta and this Chilean avenger, wild-haired and
talkative . . . Then my wife, Matilde Urrutia, said: But this is
sheer theater! . . . Theater? I said to her. And I still don't
know the answer . . . However, here you have it now . . .
Murieta is back, with a libretto and a stage . . . to tell about

rebellions and the perils of Chilean country people drawn to gold like dogs on the trail of a scent . . . tightening their belts and slaving away at one job or another for the gringo dollar . . . about lassos and bullets, or, if all else fails, a kick in the teeth . . . but still not a total loss, since there's also a love story, with verses that rhyme as they did in my palmiest days . . . and dances, with music by Sergio Ortega and Pedro Orthous, the famous theatrical director, to make his cut in the pie . . . urging this little change and that small deletion . . . and if I protested I was told the same thing had happened to Shakespeare and Lope de Vega . . . they snipped with their scissors and changed things around for your pleasure . . . After all, I am only a stage-struck apprentice . . . I gave in to everything so that Murieta could ride again . . . fly about as he might in his craziest dreams . . . on horseback with his lady-friend bandit from Chile . . . Let's hear one for Chile! . . . fly on his horse like a meteor falling to earth, coming back because I wanted it, I prodded the waiting materials, gave it all I was worth day after day there by the ocean . . . till suddenly— there was my highwayman, his horse's hoofs striking fire in the California night . . . and I said to him: Come out in the open. Come up closer . . . and he took to the road of my book and galloped off with his life and his drama, his splendor and death, like something seen in a pitiless dream . . . That's it . . . that's my song and my story . . .

Isla Negra
September 1967

Production Note

This work was first performed on October 14, 1967, in the
Teatro Antonio Varas in Santiago, Chile, by the Instituto del
Teatro of the University of Chile under the direction of Pedro
Orthous, with music by Sergio Ortega, settings by Guillermo
Núñez, costumes by Sergio Zapata, lighting by Oscar Navarro,
and choreography by Patricio Búnster, with the following cast:
Matilde Broders, María Cánepa, Bélgica Casto, Peggi
Cordero, Virginia Fischer, María Teresa Fricke, Kerry Keller,
Lina Ladrón de Guevara, Coca Mlnick, Sonia Mena, María
Angélica Núñez, Claudia Paz, Alicia Quiroga, Berta Sandoval,
Sergio Aguirre, Víctor Bogado, Jorge Boudon, Roberto Cabrera,
Franklin Caicedo, Flovio Candia, Pablo Carrillo, Alejandro
Castillo, Regildo Castro, Alejandro Cohen, Emilio Cossio,
Jacinto Cruz, Rodrigo Durán, Tennyson Ferrada, Fernando
González, Sergio Hernández, Alberto LeBrecht, Mario Lorca,
Sergio Madrid, Héctor Maglio, Sergio Montero, Alberto Rivera,
Iván Rodríguez, Andrés Rojas Murphy, Winston Rosales,
Ramón Sabat, Alejandro Salas, Alejandro Sieveking, Rubén
Sotoconil, Arturo Venegas, and Tomás Vidiella.

TRANSLATOR'S NOTE: There are two extant texts for *Ful-*
gor y muerte de Joaquín Murieta: the poet's original text, first

published by Empresa Editora Zig-Zag in 1966, and the acting
version, published by Editorial Losada in Volume II of the
third edition of *The Complete Works of Pablo Neruda* in 1968,
the text finally preferred by the poet himself. I have used
the latter as the text for this translation.

Song for a Black Singer

(NEGRO SPIRITUAL)

Down goes the river
Down to the south
I've lost my ring
I've lost my soul.

Go, sailor, go, but don't inquire
where I have hidden my own heart!
My heart is there there there
in no man's land

Down go the winds
down go the clouds
I've lost my ring
I've lost my soul.

Down goes the river
Down to the south
I'll never see again my ring, my ring,
I've for ever lost my soul, my soul.

Song for a Blond Singer

Lovely boy,
don't talk
to me!
I want to see
your daddy first!
Please call your uncle Benjamin
and your grand father Seraphim!
Lovely boy,
don't talk
to me!

I am so far
you won't believe!

I am as cold
as a star fish!

Don't talk to me
I think because
your daddy was born for me!
or your uncle Benjamin!
or your grand father Seraphim!

DATE DUE			

Neruda   225392